With love in Jesus,

THE SECRET *of*
SOUL-WINNING

THE SECRET *of* SOUL-WINNING

By

STEPHEN F. OLFORD

And they that be wise shall shine as the brightness of the firmament; and they that turn many to righteousness as the stars for ever and ever.

DANIEL 12:3

MOODY PRESS
CHICAGO

Seventh Printing, 1973

ISBN: 0-8024-7685-6

Printed in the United States of America

FOREWORD

ONCE WHEN LORD TENNYSON was on vacation in a country village he asked an old Methodist woman, "Is there any news?"

"Well," she replied, "there is only one piece of news that I know, and that is that Christ died for my sins."

Tennyson responded, "That is old news, and good news, and new news."

The chief duty and privilege of the Christian is soul-winning. The Scriptures say, "He which converteth the sinner from the error of his way shall save a soul from death, and shall hide [atone for] a multitude of sins."

There are many preachers but few soul-winners. There are many books of sermons, but few on soul-winning. In looking through the books in my library I find many books on doctrine, on Christian ethics and on homiletics; but I can count the books on soul-winning on one hand. Perhaps this neglect of the Christian's prime business is one of the causes of the church's failure to capture more men and women for Christ.

John Wesley said to his students, "You have only one business, and that is the salvation of souls."

David Brainerd at the close of his life wrote in his diary, "I cared not how I lived nor what hardships I went through if I only might gain souls for Christ."

Professor Smeaton of Edinburgh used to say to his students, "Gentlemen, reckon your ministry a failure unless souls are won to Christ."

In a day when sects are thriving because their adherents dare to take their message directly to people, the church must regain the urgency and compulsion of soul-winning, or we fight a losing battle for the minds and hearts of men.

The Rev. Stephen Olford, the distinguished pastor of Calvary Baptist Church in New York, is eminently qualified to give us helpful instruction in the art of soul-winning. Stephen Olford is not only one of the greatest Bible preachers I know but one of the most successful soul-winners I have ever met. I have been in close contact with Mr. Olford for fifteen years. We have ministered together on three continents. He is unquestionably one of the most refreshingly radiant Christians I know. He exemplifies in his personal life everything the Apostle Paul meant when he spoke of the "fruit of the Spirit." He is also a man of great compassion, carrying a burden for the lost.

In this volume Stephen Olford not only tells us what soul-winning is, but he comes directly to the point and tells us how to perform this greatest of all Christian duties.

From a heart that has been strangely and wonderfully warmed by the Spirit of God, he brings us practical suggestions about how to win men to Christ.

I am confident that no one can prayerfully read this book without being a better Christian and without being adequately equipped to convert "the sinner from the error of his way," and to save souls from death by the help of Him who loved us and gave Himself for us.

BILLY GRAHAM

CONTENTS

CHAPTER   PAGE

Foreword 5

1. Introduction 9

2. The Successful Soul-Winner 15

3. The Soul-Winner's Task 27

4. The Soul-Winner's Training 41

5. The Soul-Winner's Technique 57

6. The Soul-Winner's Target 67

7. The Soul-Winner's Travail 77

8. The Soul-Winner's Trials 89

9. The Soul-Winner's Temptations 103

10. The Soul-Winner's Triumphs 113

Bibliography 121

Chapter 1

INTRODUCTION

DOES THE SUBJECT of personal soul-winning frighten you? If it does, you have my sympathy! I say that because I know from experience what you are passing through. There was a time in my life when even the thought of talking to people, publicly or privately, paralyzed me with fear. I was not only painfully shy by nature but hopelessly indisposed to meeting new faces. Many a social occasion in our home was spoiled because of my unannounced disappearance!

The fact that I was a committed Christian did not seem to make much difference. In one sense, it made me worse. As a saved person, I knew it was my duty to witness for my Lord and, when possible, to seek to win others to Him. But such a sense of duty only brought me into inner bondage. I have known what it is to screw up my courage and walk the entire length of a train, giving out gospel booklets to anyone who was courteous enough (and, I often thought, pitying enough) to take a copy. But was I ever glad when such a task was completed!

It was not as if I had not read books on soul-winning. As it happened, I had a wide selection of works on the subject, and often I perused them in the hope of finding the secret to successful soul-winning.

Then God graciously stepped in. He had permitted me to struggle on long enough to convince me that *I* could do noth-

9

ing about it. *I* was shy; *I* was bound; and *I* was defeated. In a word, *I* was a failure.

In the first instance, divinely ordered circumstances were used to bring me out of the bondage of soul-winning *in the flesh*, into the blessing of soul-winning *in the Spirit*.

An old friend of mine whom I had not seen for years unexpectedly crossed my path. In the course of conversation, he drew my attention to an incident in the life of the saintly Oswald Chambers. Only a youth at the time, Chambers was out for a walk with a deeply taught Scottish divine. Presently a shepherd appeared from around the mountain track and would have passed the two gentlemen with little more than a word of greeting but for the intervention of Oswald. Leaving his senior friend, and stepping up to the shepherd, young Chambers pointedly asked the stranger if all were well with his soul! On the face of it, this seemed an opportunity redeemed, and a witness nobly given. But on rejoining the man of God, Oswald Chambers was met with this solemn question: "Tell me—did you get the permission of the Holy Ghost to speak to that man about his soul's welfare?"

That story started me thinking. I began to see—slowly but clearly—that SOUL-WINNING IS GOD'S WORK. From the start to the finish He must plan and carry it through. My business is to be in line with His will. Winning men and women to the Lord Jesus Christ is not a matter of trial and error but of being led by the Holy Spirit. "For as many as are led by the Spirit of God, they are the sons of God" (Romans 8:14).

Shortly after this, I was at a Deeper Life Convention. A much-used servant of God was expounding John 7:37-39. Something he said arrested me. As nearly as I can remember, these were his words: "There is only one successful Soul-Winner, and that is the Lord Jesus Christ. To try to copy Him, is to fail miserably; for His thoughts are not our

thoughts; neither are His ways our ways. If we would succeed in this great task of winning the lost to God, then
Jesus must work in us and through us, by the power of His
Spirit. Listen to His own words: 'He that believeth on me,
as the scripture hath said, out of his innermost being shall
flow rivers of living water. (This spake he of the Spirit,
which they that believe on him should receive: for the Holy
Ghost was not yet given; because that Jesus was not yet
glorified.)' Only as we believe IN Him and allow Him to
flow through us by His Spirit will men and women whom
He is drawing to Himself respond. To the Spirit-led child of
God, this will mean liberty, joy, and blessing in the work of
personal evangelism."

That evening I went home determined to cease trying and
to start trusting. From that moment soul-winning for me has
been different. Not only have I been delivered from shyness
and self-consciousness, but I have been introduced to a level
of soul-winning which is divinely directed and unspeakably
joyous.

I have failed since—many times; but always I have known
the reason—and the way of restoration! The Lord Jesus is
the only successful Soul-Winner, and it is only when He is
in complete control of my life that I can hope to share in the
fruits of His labors.

Such surrender to His sovereignty does not necessarily im-
ply or guarantee on-the-spot decisions for Christ every time
a person is approached on the subject! We certainly are
called upon to preach the gospel to *every creature;* but the
Lord adds to His Church only "such as should be [or, are
being] saved" (Acts 2:47). This is a deep mystery, but it is
a fact of Scripture and of personal experience.

What happens is that, as we witness in the power of the
Spirit to all and sundry, some soul is especially laid upon our
hearts. Like Philip of old, we are bidden (inwardly) to "go

near and join" ourselves to this person. Sometimes this results at once in a conversion. Then there are other occasions
when that honor is reserved for someone else. In either instance, however, the issue from the divine standpoint is
certain and successful. What matters supremely is that we
are "led by the Spirit of God."

"What about the person who rejects the gospel?" someone
asks. The answer to that question is treated in chapter 10,
entitled "The Soul-Winner's Triumphs." Suffice it to say here
that how a man or woman finally reacts to the offer of Christ
is none of our business. Providing we have witnessed as
faithfully as we know how, and have given the individual
concerned every opportunity to trust the Saviour, then to be
sensitive to the divine leading, we must go no further. It is
God's work, and He will be glorified in the ultimate issue.
Such an attitude ever keeps the Spirit-filled worker humble,
prayerful, and increasingly aware of the fact that he is only
an instrument to be used as and when the Master pleases.

This, then, is my testimony to God's dealings with me.
The studies that follow are but an amplification and development of this testimony. The principles outlined have been
tried and proved; therefore, they are commended with the
prayer that they may be used to lead many into the liberty
and joy of successful soul-winning.

These studies are by no means exhaustive; rather are they
intended to be suggestive. For this reason no attempt has
been made to provide the student with ready-made answers
to the problem questions that inevitably arise in the task of
evangelism. Another deliberate omission is a table of Biblical
texts that treat of doctrines and questions that the soul-
winner will have to face at one time or another. Stock answers and proof texts are adequately covered by books and
courses that have been written for that purpose, and are
obtainable from most evangelical publishers.*

*See page 121 for recommended books.

As I have implied already in an earlier paragraph, this course of simple studies has a twofold purpose: first, that of bringing all soul-winners to feel their solemn sense of responsibility to God and to the men and women they are seeking to win; and secondly, that of leading those same soul-winners into the joyous secret of moment-by-moment availability to God for the outworking of His saving plan in a world that desperately needs the gospel. If this purpose is realized in the lives of Christian workers, I know that God will be glorified; the Lord Jesus will be magnified; and I shall certainly be satisfied!

STEPHEN F. OLFORD

THE SUCCESSFUL SOUL-WINNER

Scriptures for Study

And, behold, there was a man which had his hand withered. And they asked him, saying, Is it lawful to heal on the sabbath days? that they might accuse him.

And he said unto them, What man shall there be among you, that shall have one sheep, and if it fall into a pit on the sabbath day, will he not lay hold on it, and lift it out?

How much then is a man better than a sheep? Wherefore it is lawful to do well on the sabbath days.

Then saith he to the man, Stretch forth thine hand. And he stretched it forth; and it was restored whole, like as the other.

Then the Pharisees went out, and held a council against him, how they might destroy him.

But when Jesus knew it, he withdrew himself from thence: and great multitudes followed him, and he healed them all;

And charged them that they should not make him known:

That it might be fulfilled which was spoken by Esaias the prophet, saying,

Behold my servant, whom I have chosen; my beloved, in whom my soul is well pleased: I will put my spirit upon him, and he shall show judgment to the Gentiles.

He shall not strive, nor cry; neither shall any man hear his voice in the streets.

A bruised reed shall he not break, and smoking flax shall he not quench, till he send forth judgment unto victory.

And in his name shall the Gentiles trust.

—MATTHEW 12:10-21

Chapter 2

THE SUCCESSFUL SOUL-WINNER

THE LORD JESUS CHRIST is our supreme Example in the ministry of soul-winning, as indeed He is in every other aspect of Christian life and service. We cannot study His life without being impressed with the qualifications which marked Him out as the wise Winner of souls. From the manward aspect of His life and work, soul-winning was His first concern. He could say, "The Son of man is come to seek and to save that which was lost" (Luke 19:10).

And again, "The Son of man came not to be ministered unto, but to minister, and to give his life a ransom for many" (Matthew 20:28).

The Apostle Paul later could add, "Christ Jesus came into the world to save sinners" (I Timothy 1:15).

When He taught men and women, it was with the studied object of bringing them into right relationship to God. When He healed the sick, it was in order to prepare their hearts for the experience of His forgiveness and pardon. It was just the same when He fed the crowds. The motive behind it all was to win them to Himself, as Saviour and Shepherd. The consuming passion of His soul was to seek and to save that which was lost. In every sense of the word, He was the successful Soul-Winner.

If we would be successful in soul-winning, we must needs study Him until the characteristics and spirit which marked and motivated His life are reproduced in us.

With this in mind, we wish to draw your attention to a word portrait of the perfect Soul-Winner, as given in the *Scriptures for Study*. While this passage includes a quotation from the Old Testament (Isaiah 42:1-4) which in some senses is prophetic of a day yet to come, it is at the same time a remarkable disclosure of God's perfect Servant, the Lord Jesus Christ, and therefore an abiding pattern for us.

It is important to observe that the context in which these verses are set is one of hatred, antagonism, and hostility. The Lord Jesus had just healed a man with a withered hand, with the evident intention of winning him to God. This at once aroused bitter opposition, insomuch that the Pharisees went out and held a council against Him, how they might destroy Him (v. 14).

Then follows this remarkable description of God's perfect Servant. The lesson is obvious. As soul-winners we shall ever be opposed by Satan's fierce attacks. He will never release his victims easily. Because of this, we dare not be anything less than Christlike in our reactions, or we cease to be true soul-winners.

What, then, are the characteristics of the soul-winner? Let us turn again to Matthew 12:18-21, and notice what is said of the Lord Jesus. God sets Him forth with the words, "Behold my servant."

Let us, then, behold these characteristics of the Servant of the LORD:

I. HIS APPOINTMENT

"Behold my servant, whom I have chosen" (v. 18).

All true soul-winners are divinely appointed. In the counsels of eternity the Lord Jesus was appointed to be Seeker and Saviour of men. So He came forth from the Father's side, saying, "Lo, I come: in the volume of the book it is written of me, I delight to do thy will, O my God" (Psalm 40:7-8; compare Hebrews 10:7, 9).

What was true of the Lord Jesus applies also to us. We cannot engage in this soul-winning work unless we have been divinely called and chosen.

Having called Peter, James, John, and the rest, Jesus later could say to them, "Ye have not chosen me, but I have chosen you, and ordained you, that ye should go and bring forth fruit, and that your fruit should remain" (John 15:16).

If we have heard His "Come unto me," then we must not be deaf to His "Go." His word is clear, "Go ye therefore, and make disciples of all the nations, baptizing them into the name of the Father, and of the Son and of the Holy Spirit: teaching them to observe all things whatsoever I commanded you: and lo, I am with you always, even unto the end of the world" (Matthew 28:19, 20, American Standard Version, published in 1901).

And again, "Ye shall receive power, after that the Holy Ghost is come upon you: and ye shall be witnesses unto me. . . ." (Acts 1:8).

While these words were spoken initially to the eleven disciples, the New Testament makes it plain that their application extends to Christian men and women of all time. (See Ephesians 4:7-12 and II Timothy 2:2.) The common notion that soul-winning is the exclusive work of the so-called full-time ministers of the gospel is erroneous. The Apostle Paul states quite clearly that the gift of the evangelist in the Church of Christ is "for the perfecting [or equipping] of the saints, unto the work of ministering [or serving]" (Ephesians 4:11, 12, American Standard Version). In other words, the motto and mission of every local church should be *Every-Member Evangelism.* (Note how the early disciples, having been scattered abroad because of persecution, "went everywhere preaching the word"; or, as the phrase has been freely rendered, "gossiping the gospel" (Acts 8:1, 4).

II. HIS APPROBATION

"Behold . . . my beloved, in whom my soul is well pleased. . . ." (v. 18).

Before a life can be a power for God, it must be a pleasure to God. This was always true of our Saviour, as evidenced by the Father's words of approval at the baptism and transfiguration of His well-beloved Son. (See Matthew 3:17; 17:5.) We can merit that approval only by complete submission to the Father's will. The Master could say, "I do always those things that please him" (John 8:29).

Let us never forget that the will of God is the salvation and sanctification of men and women (see I Timothy 2:3, 4 and I Thessalonians 4:3). When Jesus "must needs go through Samaria" to win a sinful woman to God, He could explain His action in the following words, "My meat is to do the will of him that sent me, and to finish his work" (John 4:34).

No wonder He merited the Father's pleasure!

III. HIS ANOINTING

"Behold my servant . . . I will put my Spirit upon him" (v. 18).

This is the anointing for service and soul-winning. It is important to recognize that there was never a moment in our Lord's experience when He was not full of the Holy Spirit. John declares, "God giveth not the Spirit by measure unto him" (John 3:34).

At the same time, while He knew the fullness of the Holy Spirit from birth, it was not until His public ministry that He experienced the anointing of the Spirit. As He stepped out of Jordan after His baptism, the Spirit came upon Him like a dove (Matthew 3:16). Later, referring to this, He could testify, "The Spirit of the Lord is upon me, because he hath anointed me to preach the gospel to the poor; he hath sent me to heal the broken-hearted, to preach deliverance to the captives, and recovering of sight to the blind, to set at liberty them that are bruised" (Luke 4:18).

Now to be successful soul-winners, we too must know not only the fullness of the Holy Spirit but this holy anointing. After Calvary, Jesus told His disciples that this anointing was the promise of His Father, and that they were to tarry in the city of Jerusalem until they were endued with power from on high (see Luke 24:49).

The word "endue" is one of rich significance. The original meaning carries the thought of being invested or clothed upon with a new power. After Pentecost, the disciples were to wear this power like a garment.

While this clothing with power took place simultaneously with the baptism, the two must not be confused. Baptism was an *immersion* in the Spirit, while the clothing with power was an *investment* of the Spirit. Baptism was initial and final (I Corinthians 12:13), while the clothing with power was initial and continual. This continual clothing with power is the result of a life of *prayerfulness* (Acts 1:14; 2:4) and *yieldedness* (Acts 5:32).

So we see that the *anointing* of the Spirit has to do particularly with service or responsibility, while the *baptism* has to do with sainthood or relationship. Later, when expanding the thought of this clothing with power, Jesus said, "Ye shall receive power, after that the Holy Ghost is come upon you: and ye shall be witnesses unto me both in Jerusalem, and in all Judea, and in Samaria, and unto the uttermost part of the earth" (Acts 1:8).

As we have seen, the *anointing* must not be confused with

the *baptism;* nor must it be regarded as synonymous with the *filling* of the Spirit. While the *baptism* has to do with relationship, and the *anointing* with responsibility, the *filling* has to do with realization. The *anointing* represents something outward, while the *filling* of the Spirit denotes an inward experience. The *anointing* is for special service, while the *filling* is for daily living.

The evidence of the anointing of the Spirit is a *spiritual authority in the work of God* and a spiritual knowledge of the Word of God. In a context where Paul is speaking of the authority of his ministry, he says, "Now he which stablisheth us with you in Christ, and hath anointed us, is God; who hath also sealed us, and given us the earnest of the Spirit in our hearts" ((II Corinthians 1:21, 22).

In the Old Testament the ceremony of anointing was related to all important offices and ministries of the servants of Jehovah. The prophet was anointed, that he might be the messenger of God to the people (I Kings 19:16). The priest was anointed, that he might be holy unto the LORD (Leviticus 8:12). The king was anointed, that the Spirit of the LORD might rest upon him in power (I Samuel 16:13). No servant of the LORD was considered qualified for his ministry without this holy anointing. Indeed, as we have seen, the Lord Jesus was anointed with the Spirit and with power at the outset of His ministry (see Acts 10:38). So Paul applies this same principle to the believers at Corinth when he reminds them that "he which . . . hath anointed us is God" (II Corinthians 1:21).

The further evidence of the anointing of the Spirit is *spiritual knowledge of the Word of God.* So the Apostle John tells us, "The anointing which ye have received of him abideth in you, and ye need not that any man teach you: but as the same anointing teacheth you of all things, and is truth, and is no lie, and even as it hath taught you, ye shall abide in him" (I John 2:27).

There is a distinct difference between "the tuition of learning and the intuition of the Spirit." One is intellectual knowledge, while the other is spiritual knowledge. While we should never undervalue the former, it is impressive to note how the Bible puts the weightier emphasis on the latter, "Eye hath not seen, nor ear heard, neither have entered into the heart of man, the things which God hath prepared for them that love him. But God hath revealed them unto us by his Spirit: for the Spirit searcheth all things, yea, the deep things of God. . . . The things of God knoweth no man, but the Spirit of God" (I Corinthians 2:9, 10).

If the soul-winner would be characterized by such spiritual authority and knowledge, he must know this anointing with the Spirit. Only thus will he be effective in his holy task of faithfully representing the living Christ.

IV. HIS ANNOUNCEMENT

"Behold my servant . . . He shall show [proclaim] judgment to the Gentiles" (v. 18).

In quoting this Old Testament passage, Matthew anticipates the preaching of the gospel to the Gentile world after Pentecost.

The word "judgment" has a wide range of meaning and includes the thought of "life-giving truths of the righteous Judge." So our message, in personal conversation or public discourse, must be that of righteousness made available through our Saviour, who is just and the Justifier of all who believe in Him (Romans 3:26).

That master soul-winner, the Apostle Paul, could announce, "I am not ashamed of the gospel of Christ: for it is the power of God unto salvation to every one that believeth. . . ." (Romans 1:16, 17).

V. HIS APPROACH

"Behold my servant. . . . He shall not strive, nor cry; neither
shall any man hear his voice in the streets. A bruised reed
shall he not break, and smoking flax shall he not quench"
(vv. 18-20).

These words describe the pervading calmness and com-
posure which characterized our Saviour's approach to men
in His work of soul-winning. Indeed, His quiet and gentle
manner so impressed itself upon the mind of the Evangelist,
that he could not help recalling Isaiah's prophecy of Him.
To Matthew, the Master's approach stood out in marked
contrast to the wrangling of the Jewish scribes; the violence
of the Roman officers; and even more, the ravings of the false
prophets and leaders of revolt, such as Judas of Galilee.
When confronted with broken and smoldering humanity,
Jesus was tender with the broken reed, and trustful with the
smoking flax. This must ever be our approach if we are to
succeed as soul-winners.

Writing to Timothy, the Apostle Paul says to him: "The
servant of the Lord must not strive; but be gentle unto all
men, apt to teach, patient" (II Timothy 2:24).

VI. HIS ASSURANCE

"Behold my servant. . . . he shall . . . send forth judgment
unto victory (vv. 18-20).

The Lord Jesus was never a pessimist or a defeatist. He
was confident of the ultimate victory of God's purpose of
grace. This secret assurance gave Him poise and positive-
ness when dealing with men and women.

Such assurance must also characterize us if we would succeed in the work of soul-winning. True love for souls "bear-
eth all things, believeth all things, hopeth all things, endur-
eth all things" (I Corinthians 13:7).

VII. HIS ACCEPTANCE

"Behold my servant. . . . in his name shall the Gentiles trust [or hope]" (vv. 18, 21).

The reality and radiance of the Saviour's faith called forth hope and trust from sin-stricken humanity. In our contact and conversation with people, we, as soul-winners, must be characterized by a reality and radiance of faith if we would have acceptance with souls who are hungry for God. It is recorded that the early disciples had favor with all the people; therefore, the Lord was able to add to the Church daily such as were being saved (see Acts 2:47).

Let us never forget that, while those who refuse the gospel may hate and persecute us, there are thousands upon thousands of men and women who respond at once to Christian reality and radiance when they encounter it.

So we have seen the sevenfold characteristics of *The Successful Soul-Winner*. If we had to copy them, what failures we should be! But, thank God, in wisdom and love He has devised a more excellent way: *it is by the power of the Lord Jesus who lives and works in and through us.*

The great apostle knew this secret, for his testimony was: "It pleased God, who separated me from my mother's womb, and called me by his grace, to reveal his Son in me, that I might preach him among the heathen. . . ." (Galatians 1:15, 16).

And again, ". . . I live; yet not I, but Christ liveth *in* me: and the life which I now live in the flesh I live by the faith of the Son of God, who loved me, and gave himself for me" (Galatians 2:20).

And yet again, ". . . we preach, warning every man, and teaching every man in all wisdom; that we may present every man perfect in Christ Jesus: whereunto I also labour, striving according to *his working*, which worketh *in* me mightily" (Colossians 1:28, 29).

If truly born again, we too have within us the wonderful secret of successful soul-winning. God's perfect Servant and Soul-Winner lives in our hearts, and longs to express Himself through our lives. Our responsibility is to recognize His indwelling Presence and then to reckon on His inexhaustible power. So shall we be able to say with the Apostle Paul: "We labour according to his working, which worketh *in* us mightily."

THE SOUL-WINNER'S TASK

Scriptures for Study

And Jesus came and spake unto them, saying, All power is given unto me in heaven and in earth.

Go ye therefore, and teach all nations, baptizing them in the name of the Father, and of the Son, and of the Holy Ghost:

Teaching them to observe all things whatsoever I have commanded you: and, lo, I am with you alway, even unto the end of the world. Amen.

—MATTHEW 28:18-20

Afterward he appeared unto the eleven as they sat at meat, and upbraided them with their unbelief and hardness of heart, because they believed not them which had seen him after he was risen.

And he said unto them, Go ye into all the world, and preach the gospel to every creature.

He that believeth and is baptized shall be saved; but he that believeth not shall be damned.

And these signs shall follow them that believe: In my name shall they cast out devils; they shall speak with new tongues;

They shall take up serpents; and if they drink any deadly thing, it shall not hurt them; they shall lay hands on the sick, and they shall recover.

So then after the Lord had spoken unto them, he was received up into heaven, and sat on the right hand of God.

And they went forth, and preached every where, the Lord working with them, and confirming the word with signs following. Amen.

—MARK 16:14-20

Chapter 3

THE SOUL-WINNER'S TASK

NEARLY TWO THOUSAND YEARS AGO, the risen Lord commissioned His disciples to "go . . . into all the world, and preach the gospel to every creature" (Mark 16:15). These words, as we observed in chapter 2, were addressed initially to the eleven disciples who represented the nucleus of the Church (see I Corinthians 15:6).

The task which the Saviour envisaged for His disciples was the evangelization of the world. The words of that commission have never been withdrawn, and the vision for world evangelization is still as clear as when the Saviour first presented it. The question arises as to how far we have fulfilled this task.

"How can such a work be attempted?" someone asks. The answer is, "By His promised power": "All power is given unto me in heaven and in earth" (Matthew 28:18). "How can such a work be accomplished?" enquires another. Our Lord replies that it is by His promised program: "Go ye therefore, and teach all nations, baptizing them in the name of the Father, and of the Son, and of the Holy Ghost: teaching them to observe all things whatsoever I have commanded you" (vv. 19, 20). "How can such a work be attested?" insists yet another. The word comes back, "By His promised Presence": "Lo, I am with you alway, even unto the end of the world" (v. 20).

It is quite evident, therefore, that the soul-winner's task is to

I. GO INTO THE WORLD WITH CHRIST'S POWER

"Jesus came and spake unto them, saying, All power is given unto me in heaven and in earth" (v. 18).

All the powers of heaven, earth, and hell are under the authority of the risen Christ. It follows that to be under His authority is to be brought into the good of that authority. None of us know the full significance of this tremendous fact. If we did, we should be witnessing greater happenings today than anything people saw when Jesus was on earth. It was the Master Himself who stated, "He that believeth on me, the works that I do shall he do also; and greater works than these shall he do; because I go unto my Father" (John 14:12).

Those first-century soul-winners took these words so seriously that in a little over thirty-three and a half years the whole of the then-known world had been evangelized. They knew that to be brought under the authority of the risen Christ was to be able to

1. Direct divine power

The Master had already promised them this power when He said, "Ye shall receive power, after that the Holy Ghost is come upon you: and ye shall be witnesses unto me both in Jerusalem, and in all Judea, and in Samaria, and unto the uttermost part of the earth" (Acts 1:8).

What is more, the disciples knew the secret of relating this divine power to any person, in any place, at any time. Observe how this is illustrated in The Acts of the Apostles:

a. *Any person* (Acts 3:1-11). Peter and John are confronted here with human need. The man, lame from his mother's womb, is a picture of helpless humanity—"shapen in iniquity" and conceived in sin (Psalm 51:5). Religion can do very little for him, for he is laid daily at the gate of the Temple which is called Beautiful, in order that he may ask alms of those who enter. Stirred with this need, Peter, supported by his fellow worker, John, fastens his eyes upon the man, and with quiet confidence says: "Silver and gold have I none; but such as I have give I thee: In the name of Jesus Christ of Nazareth rise up and walk. . . . And immediately his feet and ankle bones received strength. And he leaping up stood, and walked, and entered with them into the temple, walking, and leaping, and praising God." At the mention of the name of Jesus Christ, divine power was related to human need.

b. *Any place* (Acts 12:1-17). The voice of the gospel has been silenced; Peter is in prison. King Herod, having stretched forth his hand to vex certain of the Church, had killed James the brother of John with the sword; and then, because it pleased the Jews, he proceeded to take Peter also. God's answer to this sinister and subtle attack of the enemy was a fellowship of believers at prayer. Hear Dr. Luke's dramatic words, "Peter therefore was kept in prison: but prayer was made without ceasing of the church unto God for him" (v. 5).

Later in the chapter we read, "And his chains fell off from his hands" (v. 7).

What a demonstration of divine power!

c. *Any period* (Acts 16:16-34). It is midnight, and Paul and Silas are in the inner prison, with their feet fast in the stocks. But the record tells us they "prayed, and sang praises unto God. . . . And suddenly there was a great earthquake, so that the foundations of the prison were shaken: and immediately all the doors were opened, and every one's bands were loosed" (vv. 25, 26).

It did not matter who it was, where it was, or what it was; the power of the risen Lord was more than adequate.

This direction of divine power may or may not be accompanied by similar physical phenomena in our day; but the authority of the Lord Jesus is just the same. He is "the same yesterday, and today, and forever" (Hebrews 13:8).

Those early soul-winners knew, furthermore, that to be under the authority of the risen Christ was to be able to

2. Discipline human power

They had heard the Master say: "Whatsoever thou shalt bind on earth shall be bound in heaven: and whatsoever thou shalt loose on earth shall be loosed in heaven" (Matthew 16:19).

This power of discipline was exercised, not only in their personal lives, but also in the local church. Indeed, such was the effect of this recognized authority of Christ in the church in Jerusalem that we are told the outside world feared, and "no man . . . durst . . . join himself to them: but the people magnified them" (Acts 5:13).

Leaders within the Church had the divine authority to exercise a discipline which maintained the purity of the Christian community. Study the New Testament story and observe how sin in the Church was attacked.

a. *The sin of insincerity* (Acts 5:3, 4). Ananias and Sapphira had agreed to lie to the Church regarding their gifts. They had overlooked the solemn fact that, in wronging the Church, they were wronging God. As the representative of the Church, Peter detected this and challenged them separately with the words: "Why hath Satan filled thine heart to lie to the Holy Ghost, and to keep back part of the price of the land? . . . Thou hast not lied unto men, but unto God." The judgment of God followed, cutting off both these lives, so that "great fear came on all them that heard these things" (v. 5).

b. *The sin of immorality* (I Corinthians 5). A Christian had been involved in a scandalous disorder, such as was not even named among the Gentiles; and instead of judging this sin, the Corinthian believers were puffed up with pride and had not even mourned. So Paul had to write to them and say, "I verily, as absent in body, but present in spirit, have judged already, as though I were present, concerning him that hath so done this deed, in the name of our Lord Jesus Christ, when ye are gathered together, and my spirit, with the power of our Lord Jesus Christ, to deliver such an one unto Satan for the destruction of the flesh, that the spirit may be saved in the day of the Lord Jesus" (vv. 3-5).

And again, "Put away from among yourselves that wicked person" (v. 13).

Such was the punishment meted out to this offender that Paul had to write at a later date and tell the church at Corinth to receive back into fellowship the repentant brother, adding: "Sufficient to such a man is this punishment, which was inflicted of many" (II Corinthians 2:6).

c. *The sin of infidelity* (I Timothy 1:19, 20; II Timothy 2:17). Three men, named Hymenaeus, Alexander, and Philetus— who had made shipwreck of the faith, teaching erroneously that the resurrection was already past—had to be dealt with by the apostle; and we read that he delivered them unto Satan, that they might "learn not to blaspheme."

What solemn discipline was exercised by these men of God in the early Church! This corporate expression of such authority is only an evidence of the discipline of human power in the individual lives of these soul-winners.

Their knowledge of divine authority was such that they were able to

3. Destroy satanic power

These wise warriors of the cross were aware of the strength of the enemy. They recognized that ". . . we wrestle not against flesh and blood, but against principalities, against powers, against the rulers of the darkness of this world, against spiritual wickedness in high places" (Ephesians 6:12).

But they were also confident that ". . . the weapons of our warfare are not carnal, but mighty through God to the pulling down of strongholds . . . casting down imaginations, and every high thing that exalteth itself against the knowledge of God, and bringing into captivity every thought to the obedience of Christ" (II Corinthians 10:4, 5).

So, with certainty and victory in their hearts, they could act on the exhortation of James, the apostle, "Submit yourselves therefore to God. Resist the devil, and he will flee from you" (James 4:7).

Such resistance of the devil is dramatically illustrated in Acts 13, where we read that Paul encountered Elymas the sorcerer, who was set on thwarting the purposes of God in the preaching of the gospel. Faced with this challenge, Paul, "filled with the Holy Ghost, set his eyes on him, and said, O full of all subtilty and all mischief, thou child of the devil, thou enemy of all righteousness, wilt thou not cease to pervert the right ways of the Lord? . . . And immediately there fell on him a mist and a darkness; and he went about seeking some to lead him by the hand" (vv. 9-11).

If we would be successful soul-winners, we must always know the authority to destroy satanic power. The Apostle John tells us that ". . . for this purpose the Son of God was manifested, that he might destroy the works of the devil" (I John 3:8).

How wonderful to know that this same Lord Jesus Christ

dwells in our hearts by faith, and can therefore continue to undo the works of the devil through us, as we submit ourselves to God and "resist the devil"!

What a change would come into our personal evangelism if we knew how to direct divine power, discipline human power, and destroy satanic power! What a new sense of our high calling we should have in fulfilling the commission to go into all the world and preach the gospel to every creature!

The soul-winner's task, in the second place, is to

II. GO INTO THE WORLD WITH CHRIST'S PROGRAM

"Go ye therefore, and teach all nations, baptizing them in the name of the Father, and of the Son, and of the Holy Ghost: teaching them to observe all things whatsoever I have commanded you" (Matthew 28:19, 20).

How simple and sublime is this program—how free from all the externals and complications of ecclesiastical organizations today! You will notice that it is threefold in its demands upon the soul-winner.

To start with, the responsibility of the winner of souls is to

1. Evangelize people for Christ

"Teach [or make disciples of] all nations." This is priority number one. Men and women must be brought face to face with the risen Christ. This calls, not for education, not reformation primarily, but for evangelization. Lost sinners must be brought to the place of true repentance toward God and faith in our Lord Jesus Christ before they qualify for church membership or instruction in the deep things of God. There is a moral order here which the soul-winner must ever bear in mind. Religious leaders throughout the centuries have sought to reverse God's order, and only confusion and weakness in the life of the Church have followed.

Having evangelized men and women, the soul-winner's plain duty is then to

2. Enlist people for Christ

". . . baptizing them in the name of the Father, and of the Son, and of the Holy Ghost." Baptism is the outward sign of association with the visible Church of Christ. Once a soul-winner has led a man to the Saviour, he is responsible to God to see that the young believer is linked to a local church. The New Testament knows nothing of so-called free-lance Christianity, or church tramping. Following Peter's sermon and appeal on the Day of Pentecost ". . . they that gladly received his word were baptized: and the same day there were added unto them about three thousand souls. And they continued stedfastly in the apostles' doctrine and fellowship, and in breaking of bread, and in prayers" (Acts 2:41, 42).

Recognizing the natural tendency of men and women to neglect their church responsibilities, the writer to the Hebrews exhorts, "Let us hold fast the profession of our faith without wavering; (for he is faithful that promised;) and let us consider one another to provoke unto love and to good works: not forsaking the assembling of ourselves together, as the manner of some is; but exhorting one another: and so much the more, as ye see the day approaching" (Hebrews 10:23-25).

Thus we see that the soul-winner's task is first to evangelize people for Christ, then to enlist them, and next to

3. Edify people for Christ

". . . teaching them to observe all things whatsoever I have commanded you." A certain amount of this teaching will be done by the soul-winner himself, but naturally this will be augmented by the teaching ministry of the Church.

As we shall see in a later study, the aim of every true soul-winner is to be faithful in ". . . warning every man, and teaching every man in all wisdom; that we may present every man perfect in Christ Jesus" (Colossians 1:28).

The cause of superficiality and ignorance in the life of the Church generally is due to the negligence of this third item in the Saviour's program. As a wise winner of souls, the Apostle Paul could say when bidding farewell to the elders at Ephesus, "I have not shunned to declare unto you all the counsel of God" (Acts 20:27). That should be the pattern for every successful soul-winner.

Let us not forget, moreover, that it is for the fulfillment of this threefold program that the Lord Jesus has put His power at our disposal. He never releases power from heaven for personal aggrandizement or public exhibitionism. Without doubt, the powerlessness among churches and individual Christians at the present hour is due largely to the fact that we have substituted our own selfish interests and desires for Christ's program.

The task of the soul-winner is not only to go with Christ's power and program but, as we see from the commission, to

III. GO INTO THE WORLD WITH CHRIST'S PRESENCE

"Lo, I am with you alway, even unto the end of the world."

There is a realization of Christ's Presence which can be enjoyed only by those who personally or corporately fulfill this evangelistic commission. If you compare Matthew's account with Mark's, you will notice that the Presence of the living Lord means

1. Co-operation

"And they went forth, and preached every where, the Lord working with them" (Mark 16:20).

The apostle Paul reminds us of the power of Christ's un-

failing Presence with His own, "If God be for us, who can be
against us?" (Romans 8:31).

Even if men, ministers, or missions are not prepared to acknowledge our work in the name of the Lord, we can always
depend upon His Presence if we go forth at His bidding.
There are some pathetic words at the close of Paul's last letter
to Timothy. The apostle had been forsaken by all men, but
the old warrior had remained faithful, and his testimony in
the Roman dungeon was still clear. So it transpired that, even
in the absence of those who might have supported him, he
could confidently declare, ". . . notwithstanding the Lord
stood with me and strengthened me; that by me the preaching might be fully known, and that all the Gentiles might
hear" (II Timothy 4:17). What soul-winner can be afraid,
if he knows that the Lord is working with him?

2. Confirmation

". . . the Lord working with them, and confirming the word
with signs following." When we work with Him, He always
sees to it that there are signs following. Signs may be evidenced by attraction to Christ, or by antagonism to Christ.
As we watch the perfect Soul-Winner, especially as pictured
by the Evangelist John, we notice that every time He spoke
in private or preached in public, people took sides. They
either took up stones to stone Him, or they believed on Him.
In a similar way, the acid test of effectiveness in our soul-
winning is evidenced by the decisive impact we make upon
individuals or communities.

3. Completion

"I am with you alway [or, all the days], even unto the end
of the world [or, consummation of the age]" (v. 20). What
we begin with Him, He promises to finish, even after we have
gone on to heaven. The great apostle was confident of this

very thing, that He which had begun a good work would perform it until the day of Jesus Christ (Philippians 1:6).

What a call this is to aggressive evangelism! And what a cause this is in which to serve! It is a cause which is not temporary, but eternal; not of man's devising, but belonging to the nature of reality as revealed in Jesus Christ; a cause in which ultimate victory is assured, for its Captain has already broken through the opposing ranks and won the fight.

So He bids all true soul-winners to rally under His banner, and go into the world with His power, His program, and His Presence. Nothing less than this is the task of the successful soul-winner.

THE SOUL-WINNER'S TRAINING

Scriptures for Study

Wherefore he saith, When he ascended up on high, he led captivity captive, and gave gifts unto men.

(Now that he ascended, what is it but that he also descended first into the lower parts of the earth?

He that descended is the same also that ascended up far above all heavens, that he might fill all things.)

And he gave some, apostles; and some, prophets; and some, evangelists; and some, pastors and teachers;

For the perfecting of the saints, for the work of the ministry, for the edifying of the body of Christ:

Till we all come in the unity of the faith, and of the knowledge of the Son of God, unto a perfect man, unto the measure of the stature of the fullness of Christ:

That we henceforth be no more children, tossed to and fro, and carried about with every wind of doctrine, by the sleight of men, and cunning craftiness, whereby they lie in wait to deceive;

But speaking the truth in love, may grow up into him in all things, which is the head, even Christ:

From whom the whole body fitly joined together and compacted by that which every joint supplieth, according to the effectual working in the measure of every part, maketh increase of the body unto the edifying of itself in love.

—EPHESIANS 4:8-16

Study to show thyself approved unto God, a workman that needeth not to be ashamed, rightly dividing the word of truth.

—II TIMOTHY 2:15

39

But continue thou in the things which thou hast learned and hast been assured of, knowing of whom thou hast learned them;

And that from a child thou hast known the holy scriptures, which are able to make thee wise unto salvation through faith which is in Christ Jesus.

All scripture is given by inspiration of God, and is profitable for doctrine, for reproof, for correction, for instruction in righteousness:

That the man of God may be perfect, throughly furnished unto all good works.

—II TIMOTHY 3:14-17

Chapter 4

THE SOUL-WINNER'S TRAINING

The soul-winner's training must be viewed as threefold:

I. SPIRITUAL TRAINING

When the Lord Jesus appointed His twelve disciples to the ministry of soul-winning. ". . . he ordained twelve, that they should be with him, and that he might send them forth to preach" (Mark 3:14).

You will notice that He did not send them forth at once, even though Andrew and Philip seemed to be natural soul-bringers from the very start. For three and a half years the Master trained His men—by instruction, by discipline, and by example—in order that He might send them forth to be witnesses unto Him to the far ends of the earth.

Only by being with the Lord Jesus shall we come to know what is involved in

1. The soul-winner's obligation

Turn to Romans 1:14-16, and see how this sense of obligation expressed itself in the life and language of the Apostle Paul. He could say, "I am debtor both to the Greeks, and to the Barbarians; both to the wise, and to the unwise. So, as much as in me is, I am ready to preach the gospel to you that are at Rome also. For I am not ashamed of the gospel of Christ: for it is the power of God unto salvation to every one that believeth; to the Jew first, and also to the Greek."

41

Paul viewed men and women—irrespective of their race, rank, or religion—as his creditors; and he was ever restless until his debt to them was fully discharged. His sense of obligation is summed up in three short sentences: "I am debtor"; "I am ready"; and "I am not ashamed."

Writing to the church at Corinth, he expresses a similar burden when he states, "Though I preach the gospel, I have nothing to glory of: for necessity is laid upon me; yea, woe is unto me, if I preach not the gospel!" (I Corinthians 9:16).

Paul had a message which burned within him, and wherever he went he had to offer Christ to the people. This sense of obligation has characterized all the great soul-winners and evangelists throughout the history of the Church. It is said of D. L. Moody that he rarely went to bed a happy man if he had not talked to someone during the day about the Lord Jesus Christ.

2. The soul-winner's education

Addressing future soul-winners, Jesus said, "Come ye after me, and I will make you to become fishers of men" (Mark 1:17).

Only by spending time alone with Jesus shall we learn the divine art of soul-winning. There is no better way of doing this than by reading, studying, and inwardly digesting the four Gospels. In examining the interviews recorded, especially by Matthew (some sixteen), and John (some seventeen), we may learn that

a. *Soul-winning is a priority work for every Christian.* As the master Soul-Winner, the Lord Jesus could declare, "The Son of man is come to seek and to save that which was lost" (Luke 19:10). That was His supreme passion, to seek and to save the individual. A vivid illustration of His thought and care is given in that story which John records in his Gospel, chap-

ter four. No one can read those opening verses without being
impressed with the little word "must": "He must needs go
through Samaria" (v. 4). The seeking and saving of this lost
soul was a divine imperative, even though it meant a detour
of some miles, involving weariness, hunger, and thirst. It was
a priority item in his program for that day.

The Master was possessed by a sense of being sent, or commissioned, to bring men and women to God. Before He left
His disciples to go to heaven, He said to them, as He says to
us today, "As my Father hath sent me, even so send I you"
(John 20:21).

b. *Soul-winning is a perennial work for every Christian.* Writing to Timothy, Paul exhorts him to "preach the word; be instant in season, out of season. . . ." (II Timothy 4:2). How
often this phrase is quoted, "Be instant in season and out of
season"! In point of fact, however, there is no "and" in this
injunction. The whole point of the apostle's command is to
show that there is no "out of season" time for the true soul-
winner. The sense implicit in the words is this: "Take opportunity, or make it." Formal preaching may have to be re-
stricted to a traditional program, but witnessing and soul-
winning are a responsibility to which we are committed at
any time of day or night.

Nicodemus could go and find the Lord Jesus available and
ready to speak to him in the night watches; while the woman
of Samaria was dealt with at noonday, when most people
would be seeking the shade of their homes. Our Christian
witness and soul-winning should be like "a tree planted by
the rivers of water, that bringeth forth his fruit in his season;
his leaf also shall not wither; and whatsoever he doeth shall
prosper" (Psalm 1:3). God make us evergreen trees and perennial fruit-bearers.

c. *Soul-winning is a productive work for every Christian.* We are commissioned to "preach the gospel to every creature" (Mark 16:16). No other method reaches *all* classes. Anyone knows that there are some people who will never be reached except through personal contact. In the normal course of events, they would not attend a church service or an evangelistic rally; yet they are souls for whom Christ died.

What is more, personal work always produces the best results. There is no comparison between what may be accomplished through public preaching and personal soul-winning.

It was Dean Inge who distinguished public preaching from personal soul-winning when he remarked: "Preaching is like taking a bucket of water and throwing it over a number of open-necked bottles; whereas personal soul-winning is taking each bottle to the tap and filling it."

C. H. Spurgeon used to say: "Hand-picked fruit for me every time!"

Preaching might be likened to shaking a tree in order to harvest the fruit. The fruit falls all right, but so often with resultant bruising and damage. Personal soul-winning, on the other hand, is like taking a ladder and climbing into the tree to reach and pick the fruit carefully and successfully.

Have you ever thought of the difference it would make to the true Church if every Christian won three souls to Christ each year? Consider this mathematically for a moment. If there were only five thousand Christians in the world, and each one led three souls to Christ in a year (and each succeeding year), and also taught his converts to do the same—in one year there would be twenty thousand Christians; in nine years there would be over one thousand millions; and in ten years the whole of the known world would be evangelized!

Such, then, are some of the lessons that emerge as we learn of Christ, the successful Soul-Winner.

3. The soul-winner's motivation

Fellowship with the Lord Jesus in the ministry of soul-winning begets in us

a. *A true concern for souls.* We have already observed something of the Saviour's interest in, and concern for, individual men and women. Perhaps the most telling picture He gives of Himself is that of the Shepherd seeking the lost sheep, "How think ye? if a man have an hundred sheep, and one of them be gone astray, doth he not leave the ninety and nine, and goeth into the mountains, and seeketh that which is gone astray? And if so be that he find it, verily I say unto you, he rejoiceth more of that sheep, than of the ninety and nine which went not astray" (Matthew 18:12, 13).

With the true concern for souls, fellowship with the Master begets in us

b. *A true compassion for souls.* We read that "when he saw the multitudes, he was moved with compassion on them, because they fainted, and were scattered abroad, as sheep having no shepherd" (Matthew 9:36). It is not sufficient to have a sense of obligation. There must be a spirit of motivation. Only the love of Christ can constrain us, that is, press us into action, narrow us down to irresistible and inescapable obedience (II Corinthians 5:14).

4. The soul-winner's operation

The Master's soul-winning operations were always God-planned and Spirit-controlled; and so should ours be if we are to know anything of the conscious fullness of the Holy Spirit in our lives. Only when the Spirit of God operates within us can we know

a. *The contact that is planned by God.* We are told that "as many as are led by the Spirit of God, they are the sons of

God" (Romans 8:14). If only we knew this leading of the Spirit more often and more deeply, we should never make the tragic mistakes in our work of soul-winning. While we are to be "instant in season, out of season" in all our work of personal evangelism, this in no way implies indiscriminate approaches to unprepared men and women. Not for one moment do we imagine that our Lord's contacts were indiscriminate and unprepared. He, who was so led by the Spirit of God, was always making contacts that were planned in heaven. To discover this secret is to be delivered from the bondage and boredom of unsuccessful soul-winning in the energy of the flesh, and to be brought into the blessing of God-planned contacts that ultimately lead to conversions.

b. *The conversation that is prepared by God.* If we are led by the Spirit of God, then it follows that we shall know the liberty of the Holy Spirit, for "where the Spirit of the Lord is, there is liberty" (II Corinthians 3:17). How often is this illustrated throughout the New Testament! Paul tells us that to be filled with the Holy Spirit is to be able to speak, sing, and submit! (Ephesians 5:18-21). Peter and the rest of the disciples could pray, and even minister the Word of God to one another; but they were incapable of witnessing and soul-winning until they were full of the Holy Spirit (see Acts 1 and 2). The secret of liberated conversation is the conscious fullness of the Holy Spirit.

c. *The conviction that is produced by God.* This point is vital. Before the Lord Jesus left His disciples, He said, "If I depart, I will send him [the Comforter] unto you. And when he is come, he will reprove [or, convict] the world of sin, and of righteousness, and of judgment: of sin, because they believe not on me; of righteousness, because I go to my Father, and ye see me no more; of judgment, because the prince of this world is judged" (John 16:7-11).

It is amazing how many Christians fail to realize that the Holy Spirit operates through God's people in this work of conviction. This is true in individual work, as well as in the corporate witness of the Church. When the Holy Spirit fills our lives, magnifying and glorifying the Lord Jesus in our mortal bodies, the outside world becomes aware of the damning sin of unbelief.

d. *The conversion that is purposed by God.* Of the early Church it is said that "the Lord added . . . daily such as should be [or, were being] saved" (Acts 2:47). No conversion happens by chance. The whole movement is divinely controlled. "No man can come unto me, except the Father which hath sent me draw him" (John 6:44).

What a holy joy and privilege to be caught up in this redemptive purpose, and to co-operate with God the Father, God the Son, and God the Holy Spirit, in a work of genuine conversion!

This, then, is the soul-winner's operation: contact, then conversation, followed by conviction, consummating in conversion—all governed by the operation of the Holy Spirit.

5. The soul-winner's intercession

Prayer should precede, accompany, and follow every phase of this holy task of winning men and women to a personal knowledge of Christ.

As we shall see in a future study, only by our travailing in prayer can souls be born into the family of God. "Pray without ceasing" (I Thessalonians 5:17) might well be the soul-winner's motto. This not only means the *activity* of prayer, as the Christian worker wrestles with God for the salvation of men and women, but the *attitude* of prayer at all times.

When the Apostle lays bare his heart concerning his burden for unconverted Israel, he says, "Brethren, my heart's desire and prayer to God for Israel is that they might be saved" (Romans 10:1). Prayerfulness and fruitfulness are inseparable. Let every soul-winner remember that.

II. BIBLICAL TRAINING

Biblical training should include

1. Memorizing the Bible

David could say, "Thy word have I hid in mine heart, that I might not sin against thee" (Psalm 119:11).

The value of memorizing the Word of God cannot be over-stressed. The soul-winner will be hampered again and again if his memory is not well stored with passages from the Word of God that are likely to be of use to him in leading men and women to a personal knowledge of Christ.

It has now been established by psychologists that memorizing does not depend so much on whether a person has a so-called good memory or bad memory, and that this applies to both young and old. The secret lies in four simple principles, which can be related to the memorizing of the Bible, as well as poetry, prose, or anything else.

a. *Concentration.* This presupposes interest, desire, discipline, and hard work. Most people who cannot memorize Scripture are not interested and certainly not desirous of doing so. But, given these first two essentials, there must be the discipline and hard work of learning by heart such selected passages as will best aid the soul-winner in his task.

b. *Meditation.* One of the best ways of impressing the Scriptures upon the mind is this mental exercise known as meditation. It denotes the turning over in the mind of a verse or passage until it is understood and enjoyed. It is easier to remember words that are understood and enjoyed than those that are merely learned in parrot-like fashion.

c. *Repetition.* At regular intervals, all passages memorized should be reviewed. By this process of repetition, deeper impressions are made upon the mind.

d. *Application.* Yet one more way of assisting the memory to retain what is learned is the personal application of the Word of God. Indeed, only as truth is personally applied does it become to us "the sword of the Spirit" (Ephesians 6:17). The Holy Scriptures must live for us if they are to be effective in our ministry of soul-winning.

If and when we have given ourselves wholly to this discipline of memorizing the Scriptures—by concentration, meditation, repetition, and application—then, and only then, are we qualified to trust the Holy Spirit to bring to our remembrance whatsoever God has said to us. (See John 14:26.)

2. Marking the Bible

Methods of marking the Bible are numerous. The soul-winner will decide which one serves his purpose best. It is valuable, however, for him to develop a system of cross-reference marking, to enable him to turn from one subject to another with ease and absence of any embarrassment.

To illustrate a simple method which we have often used, seven steps in God's way of salvation are listed below. All that the soul-winner needs to remember is the first reference; thereafter, by a system of cross-references noted in the margin of his Bible, he can follow through the seven steps as here outlined.

a. *The need of salvation* (Romans 3:23; 6:23)

b. *The cost of salvation* (I Corinthians 15:3, 4; Romans 4:25; 5:6-8)

c. *The way of salvation* (Acts 16:31; John 1:12)

d. *The joy of salvation* (Romans 10:9, 10. Illustrate with Acts 2:41; 8:37, 39.)

e. *The terms of salvation* (Luke 14:26-33)

f. *The act of salvation* (John 1:12; 5:24; Revelation 3:20)

g. *The seal of salvation* (John 10:28-30; Ephesians 1:13, 14)

Needless to say, for each of these steps more references might be cited; but these will suffice to show how, by cross-reference marking, any subject or doctrine in the Word of God can be traced out in order of sequence.

3. Mastering the Bible

One of the dangers of memorizing, or even marking, the Bible is that of acquiring superficial knowledge. Someone has said that a text out of context is a pretext! How often verses or passages of Scripture are quoted to support arguments or doctrines with which they are not even remotely connected!

The soul-winner must study to show himself "approved unto God, a workman that needeth not to be ashamed, rightly dividing the word of truth" (II Timothy 2:15).

This will involve studying (or being diligent)

a. *To prove the Word of God.* One "approved unto God," simply interpreted, means one who has tested and proved the Word of God by trial and experience; or, in other words, one who has practiced the Word of God to the approval of God.

From the general teaching of the Bible, we learn that there are two ways in which the Word of God can be practiced to the approval of God:

(1) *Obediently.* Samuel reminds us that "to obey is better than sacrifice, and to hearken than the fat of rams" (I Samuel 15:22; see also Jeremiah 11:3). Without due attention to this essential, it is perilously easy to find one's self practicing the Word of God selfishly, heretically, or formally.

(2) *Overcomingly.* John, writing to young men, says: "Ye are strong, and the word of God abideth in you, and ye have

overcome the wicked one" (I John 2:14). When the Word is practiced obediently, it issues in an overcoming life. How beautifully this is demonstrated in the life of our Lord, who obeyed the Word and overcame by the Word.

There will also be studying

b. *To prize the Word of God,* "a workman that needeth not to be ashamed." This follows in perfect order, for a workman is never ashamed of that which has been tried and proved to be effective in his own life. And so he prizes the Word of God

(1) *Lovingly.* With the psalmist he can say, "O how love I thy law! it is my meditation all the day" (Psalm 119:97).

(2) *Loyally.* Solomon once wrote, "Buy the truth, and sell it not" (Proverbs 23:23).

And later Jude exhorted all true lovers of the Word of God, saying, "Earnestly contend for the faith which was once delivered unto the saints" (Jude 3).

You can test the measure of your love and loyalty to the Word of God by asking yourself what you have sacrificed for the knowledge of the truth. A man cannot spend time, suffer persecution, and stand firm to buy the truth, and then prize it lightly enough to sell it. An unashamed workman will never sell his tools.

Again, there will be studying

c. *To preach the Word of God,* "rightly dividing the word of truth." Until it is proved and prized, the Bible cannot be preached. The man who knows what it is to work it out in daily life, and to prize it above all else; will know how rightly to divide the Word of truth. Paul's expression here carries the thought of preaching the Word

(1) *Courageously.* Bengel takes Paul to mean that Timothy must make a straight way for the Word of truth, and must

himself walk straight forward according to this line, turning neither to the right nor to the left. The preaching of this order must be fearless and courageous. It cannot deviate for anyone, or at any cost.

It will be remembered that the apostle in another way encourages the young man Timothy to be fearless in his preaching, teaching "no other doctrine" (I Timothy 1:3).

(2) *Clearly.* Some commentators remark that "rightly dividing" is a metaphor used for "laying out a road," thus implying a clear pathway to a destination. Such preaching leaves no doubt in the hearer's mind as to the point of truth in view. The Levites of Nehemiah's day were preachers of this kind (see Nehemiah 8:8).

(3) *Conveniently.* There are still others who maintain that the metaphor is that of a father or steward who is cutting and distributing bread at the table. Solomon, in the book of Proverbs, sums up this convenient preaching when he prays, "Feed me with food convenient for me" (Proverbs 30:8).

Paul puts it another way when he exhorts Timothy to "reprove, rebuke, exhort with all longsuffering and doctrine"—according to the specific need (II Timothy 4:2).

In order to prove, prize, and preach the Word of God worthily, we must seek not only to master the Bible but also to be mastered by it. Only thus shall we be qualified to rightly divide the Word of truth.

III. PRACTICAL TRAINING

There are three aspects of practical training which must be studied and practiced:

1. The art of presentability

Research on this holy work of winning men and women to Jesus Christ has revealed, to an alarming degree, just how important is the Christian's presentability. It is amazing—as well as serious—how many potential evangelistic contacts with unbelievers are thwarted by the extremes in the Christian's presentability.

On the one hand, there are those who follow the fashions of the world so closely as to become as sophisticated as the people they are striving to win. The unbeliever expects to see a difference, both in a Christian's appearance and in his approach.

Then there are those who go to the other extreme of being so careless and frumpish that they lose their opportunity with the outsider.

Appearance, apparel, and approach do matter, even though it might be argued that God can work in spite of these things. Were evidence necessary, it could be proved beyond doubt how important are such matters as cleanliness, tidiness and neatness of appearance, and pleasantness of approach.

Writing to Timothy, the experienced apostle exhorts, "Let no man despise thy youth; but be thou an example of the believers, in word, in conversation [or manner of life], in charity, in spirit, in faith, in purity" (I Timothy 4:12).

And again, to Titus, "In all things showing thyself a pattern of good works: in doctrine showing uncorruptness, gravity, sincerity, sound speech, that cannot be condemned; that he that is of the contrary part may be ashamed, having no evil thing to say of you" (Titus 2:7, 8).

Writing to the women, Paul adds, ". . . in like manner also, that women adorn themselves in modest apparel, with shamefacedness and sobriety; not with broided [that is, braided] hair, or gold, or pearls, or costly array; but (which becometh women professing godliness) with good works" (I Timothy 2:9, 10).

Let us never forget that we are called upon to "adorn the doctrine of God our Saviour in all things" (Titus 2:10). Only

as we are Spirit-filled shall we know the modesty, balance,
and presentability which become the gospel we represent.

2. The art of sociability

One of the outstanding characteristics of the life of our Lord
Jesus Christ was His sociability. The rich and the poor, the
good and the bad, the young and the old, were all alike at-
tracted to Him. Luke tells us that publicans and sinners drew
near unto Him to hear Him, and the Pharisees and scribes
unwittingly paid Him a compliment when they murmured,
saying: "This man receiveth sinners, and eateth with them"
(Luke 15:1, 2).

Even the Master Himself quotes His enemies, when they
say of Him: "Behold . . . a friend of publicans and sinners!"
(Luke 7:34).

There was a holy, healthy magnetism about His personality, which drew to Him all who were in need. It is recorded
that "they came to him from every quarter" (Mark 1:45).

Conservatism, self-consciousness, and snobbishness are fa-
tal in the work of soul-winning. Nothing less than the out-
living of the indwelling attractiveness and friendliness of the
Lord Jesus will succeed in personal evangelism. The soul-
winner must diligently study and practice the art of sociability. Day-by-day contacts in the home, in the church, and
in the business world provide ample opportunity and scope
for this. It has been said that if we would win some, we
must be winsome.

3. The art of adaptability

A passage to which we must return again and again in these
studies is I Corinthians 9:19-22. The apostle sums it up when
he says, "I am made all things to all men, that I might by all
means save some" (v. 22).

We only have to follow this great soul-winner in his evangelistic itineraries to see how he translated these principles into action. For every changing situation there was a different approach.

The same, of course, is true of the Master Himself. He could adapt Himself in such a way as to take full advantage of every opportunity to preach the good news. He could turn a fishing boat into a pulpit, a well-side into a counseling room, and the everyday happenings around Him into object lessons and topics of soul-winning conversation.

Adaptability presupposes a good grasp of general knowledge and close observation of the ways of men and women in the world. It suggests also alertness and anticipation in the course of one's normal vocations and activities. It is an art which must be cultivated, and then employed to the best advantage.

So we have seen what training involves. It behooves the soul-winner to become as proficient as he possibly can in all three aspects—spiritual, Biblical, and practical.

Needless to say, no one can ever claim that he has finally attained or completely qualified. The whole of life will have to be devoted to the development of knowledge and enrichment of experience in this greatest of all tasks—that of winning men and women to our Lord Jesus Christ.

THE SOUL-WINNER'S TECHNIQUE

Scriptures for Study

For though I preach the gospel, I have nothing to glory of: for necessity is laid upon me; yea, woe is unto me, if I preach not the gospel!

For if I do this thing willingly, I have a reward: but if against my will, a dispensation of the gospel is committed unto me.

What is my reward then? Verily that, when I preach the gospel, I may make the gospel of Christ without charge, that I abuse not my power in the gospel.

For though I be free from all men, yet have I made myself servant unto all, that I might gain the more.

And unto the Jews I became as a Jew, that I might gain the Jews; to them that are under the law, as under the law, that I might gain them that are under the law;

To them that are without law, as without law, (being not without law to God, but under the law to Christ,) that I might gain them that are without law.

To the weak became I as weak, that I might gain the weak: I am made all things to all men, that I might by all means save some.

—I CORINTHIANS 9:16-22

Chapter 5

THE SOUL-WINNER'S TECHNIQUE

IT MUST BE RECOGNIZED that no rigid rule can be laid down for personal soul-winning; or, indeed, for any other form of Christian service. God is sovereign in His work and never deals with any two people in exactly the same way. If for that reason alone, the soul-winner should be prepared always to follow God's leading rather than his own methods and techniques, however well they may have been tried and proved.

Having said that cautionary word, we would consider technique in soul-winning in three movements:

I. THE APPROACH

Assuming that the soul-winner is always on the alert for opportunities for personal evangelism, his contact with people may well be along any one of the following approaches:

1. The shock approach

This must always be used with care. It denotes a sudden approach to a person, broaching the subject of his soul's welfare at once.

There were occasions when our Lord used this method, but careful study will show that the circumstances and people concerned justify His approach every time. Think, for instance, of the words He used when addressing an eminent theologian of His day, as recorded in John, chapter three.

There is nothing in the story that would lead us to believe that there was any gradual build-up to the Saviour's abrupt statements, "Verily, verily, I say unto thee, Except a man be born again, he cannot see the kingdom of God. . . . Verily, verily, I say unto thee, Except a man be born of water and of the Spirit, he cannot enter into the kingdom of God" (vv. 3, 5).

In fact, on the surface, it would appear that His approach was quite unrelated to Nicodemus' introductory remarks.

The shock approach, in special instances, may well be the Holy Spirit's means of awakening to a sense of need a person to whom the gospel has been presented already, but who has given little evidence of being either interested or concerned.

The kind of questions asked on these occasions will be well known by the experienced soul-winner. For example: "Are you saved?" "Have you been born again?" "Have you a living experience of the Lord Jesus Christ?"

2. The gentle approach

This signifies the winning of the individual through deeds of kindness; studied points of common interest, for example, the same job, similar hobbies, and so on; and the kind of friendliness to all people, in all circumstances, that becomes a disciple of " the friend of sinners."

3. The conversational approach

This is a method which must be diligently cultivated by the soul-winner. Experience has proved that, once a conversation begins, there are very few topics which cannot be turned to serve the ultimate aim of presenting the gospel.

To be a good conversationalist, the soul-winner must study to be well-informed, sociable, and adaptable. He must keep abreast of public news, contemporary life, and modern thought. At school we were advised never to contemplate house-to-house evangelism, or a preaching trek, without first reading through the current issues of the public press and popular magazines, giving attention especially to politics, sports, fashions and general news. Nothing causes an outsider to lose interest more quickly than the evidence in a soul-winner of unrelatedness to contemporary life and ignorance of public affairs. The impression he gets at once is that here is a man whose Christianity does not work in everyday life.

4. The literature approach

The soul-winner must carry with him at all times well-written and tastefully produced booklets and tracts. As opportunities present themselves, the appropriate piece of literature should be offered to the individual, with a prayer that it may lead to a worthwhile talk. It is of first importance that the soul-winner should be familiar with the contents of each booklet or tract, and know how to answer the type of question which might naturally arise from the reading of the literature.

The possibilities of tract distribution are beyond all computation. To illustrate this, Brigadier H. Pimm Smith tells of a certain Joseph Barr, who was a young clerk in a small Scottish town. "At the home of the aged couple with whom he boarded, the young man one day saw a copy of *The War Cry* which had been left there. The old people asked Mr. Barr to read it to them. As he read the paper, he was gripped by its contents. On the back page he saw an advertisement of some of Catherine Booth's books: *Aggressive Christianity, What Doth Hinder?* and a penny pamphlet on *Holiness*. The young man sent for the books. The reading of them gave him a troubled conscience and some sleepless nights. After being in a state of deep conviction for a week, he yielded himself to God and vowed that he would wear a Salvation Army uniform, that he was willing to become an officer and, if necessary, go on overseas service for the King of kings."

Lieutenant-Commissioner Barr (R), that one-time clerk, went to be with Christ; but in the intervening years he had served in Britain, Canada, Newfoundland, the West Indies, and Korea. His wife died in Peking some years ago, but they left three daughters who are serving as Salvation Army majors: one in a Canadian hospital, a second in Germany, and a third in New York. What a fruitful harvest from the sowing of a penny copy of *The War Cry* and a few books!

Some one else has pointed out that a tract is dynamic, because it is as powerful as the Word of God which it carries. It is versatile, because it can be used in many ways. It is timeless, because it never loses its vitality: it never dies. It is safe, because it will never confuse or garble its message. It will speak without fear or favor. It is universal, because there is no language in which it cannot bring its message. It takes no account of race, color, or condition of life, being as much at home in a wretched hovel as in a gilded palace. It is convenient, because it is easily procured and easily passed on to others. All that a tract requires is that willing hands bring it into contact with human souls.

5. The after-meeting approach

This is the introduction to soul-winning which is often unused or misused, but which none the less provides the most fruitful opportunities for winning men and women to Christ. At the close of an evangelistic meeting, the soul-winner should keep a careful lookout for any who may be open to the gospel message. Without appearing to be an observer, the soul-winner should watch for the person who lingers at the back of the auditorium or church, or who wistfully looks around to catch the eye of the speaker, or who shows evident signs of conviction and brokenness. Avoiding tactless buttonholing, the winner of souls should approach such an individual and pleasantly introduce himself by saying: "Good evening: so nice to

does not know the simple steps into the experience of salvation. There is no greater joy, albeit a solemn responsibility, for the soul-winner than to be confronted with a genuinely serious sinner. His procedure constitutes our next point.

III. THE APPEAL

The analysis of the spiritual state of the seeker will determine the kind of appeal to win the soul. Each category will require its own treatment. Basically, however, the aim is to win the mind, heart, and will.

To achieve this, it is necessary to present the gospel in order to

1. Satisfy the mind

This leads the seeker to say, "I must be saved." It requires a reasonable presentation of the truth. At this stage, therefore, it is possible—as well as wise—to convey the truth without necessarily turning to Scriptural passages. This approach might well be supported also by the experience and testimonies of respected and well-known Christian men and women.

2. Stir the heart

This leads the seeker to say, "I can be saved." Here it is essential to use the Word of God, so that the faith of the individual does not stand in the wisdom of men, but in the power of God (I Corinthians 2:5). Nothing stirs the heart like the Word of God rightly interpreted and applied. (The seven steps in the way of salvation, given in Unit 4, might be applied here.)

3. Strengthen the will

This gets the seeker to say, "I will be saved." This is the personal and practical response. The soul-winner's solemn responsibility at this point is to lead the seeker to repent toward God and exercise faith in the Lord Jesus Christ, as Sin-Bearer, Saviour, and Sovereign.

To crystalize his act of faith, it is helpful to invite audible prayer. It depends largely on the seeker's background and capabilities as to whether he should be asked to pray in his own words, or repeat a simple form of response suggested by the soul-winner. Much discernment and prayerfulness are needed here, so as to obviate embarrassment and confusion. A simple prayer which the soul-winner may well use is suggested here:

"Realizing that I am a sinner, and believing that the Lord Jesus Christ died to put away my sin, and rose again to justify me, I now receive Him as my personal Saviour and acknowledge Him as Lord of my life."

Supporting Scriptural references are as follows, "For all have sinned, and come short of the glory of God" (Romans 3:23). "Jesus our Lord . . . was delivered for our offences, and was raised again for our justification" (Romans 4:24, 25). "But as many as received him, to them gave he power to become the sons of God, even to them that believe on his name" (John 1:12). "If thou shalt confess with thy mouth the Lord Jesus, and shalt believe in thine heart that God hath raised him from the dead, thou shalt be saved" (Romans 10:9).

Whether or not the soul-winner kneels for prayer with the seeker must be a matter of individual judgment and decision, in the light of the circumstances and persons concerned. What must be emphasized again is that on no account should the seeker be offended or insulted in any way whatsoever.

Having led him to receive Christ, the soul-winner should now teach him to seek

a. *Communion with the Lord*—by systematically reading His Word, spending time in prayer, and identifying himself with the fellowship of a local, Christ-exalting church. (See Matthew 4:4; Luke 18:1; Hebrews 10:25.)

b. *Cleansing from the Lord,* when sin is committed. (See I John 1:9.)

c. *Confession of the Lord*—by trusting Him, as the indwelling Christ, to live and speak through him in every circle of life. (See Galatians 2:20; Philippians 1:21; 4:13.)

God ever make us "wise as serpents, and harmless as doves" in our ministry of personal soul-winning (Matthew 10:16).

THE SOUL-WINNER'S TARGET

Scriptures for Study

And you, that were sometime alienated and enemies in your mind by wicked works, yet now hath he reconciled
In the body of his flesh through death, to present you holy and unblameable and unreproveable in his sight:

If ye continue in the faith grounded and settled, and be not moved away from the hope of the gospel, which ye have heard, and which was preached to every creature which is under heaven; whereof I Paul am made a minister;

Who now rejoice in my sufferings for you, and fill up that which is behind of the afflictions of Christ in my flesh for his body's sake, which is the church:

Whereof I am made a minister, according to the dispensation of God which is given to me for you, to fulfil the word of God;

Even the mystery which hath been hid from ages and from generations, but now is made manifest to his saints:

To whom God would make known what is the riches of the glory of this mystery among the Gentiles; which is Christ in you, the hope of glory:

Whom we preach, warning every man, and teaching every man in all wisdom; that we may present every man perfect in Christ Jesus:

Whereunto I also labour, striving according to his working, which worketh in me mightily.

—Colossians 1:21-29

Chapter 6

THE SOUL-WINNER'S TARGET

WHEN JESUS SENT FORTH HIS APOSTLES to evangelize the world, He did not commission them to secure decisions, but rather to make disciples of all nations (see Matthew 28:19). And the soul-winner today does not fulfill his task if he does not keep that target or goal before him.

The evangelistic *objective* should be nothing less than a perfect manhood in Christ, since He is the only hope of the world now and in the age to come. Thus the Apostle Paul could say: "We preach, warning every man, and teaching every man in all wisdom; that we may present every man perfect in Christ Jesus."

In the *Suggested Scriptures for Study* we are clearly shown

I. THE MEANS OF ACHIEVING THIS TARGET

"Christ . . . whom we preach" (Colossians 1:27, 28). The soul-winner can never be successful in this ministry unless he aims at perfection. So the objective must ever be to make men and women like Christ.

To achieve this aim, the soul-winner must faithfully present twin truths concerning the Lord Jesus:

1. Christ for us

See Colossians 1:20, 21. Notice also I Corinthians 1 and 2:2. The convert must be grounded and settled in the great doctrines that center in the work of Christ on the cross, that is, Christ for us.

To illustrate this, consider the benefits of the work which Christ accomplished at Calvary, as found in this chapter alone (Colossians 1). We are told that through the cross we have

a. *Redemption.* ". . . in whom we have redemption through his blood" (v. 14). Unlike any other death, Christ's outpoured life paid the ransom price for sinners who were in the slave market of sin.

b. *Forgiveness.* ". . . in whom we have . . . forgiveness of sins" (v. 14). By virtue of Christ's substitutionary sacrifice, the believer's sins can be removed ". . . as far as the east is from the west" (Psalm 103:12)—the place of NO RETURN. ". . . behind" God's "back" (Isaiah 38:17)—the place of NO REMEMBRANCE. ". . . into the depths of the sea" (Micah 7:19)—the place of NO RECOVERY.

No other death could have accomplished this.

c. *Peace.* ". . . having made peace through the blood of his cross" (v. 20); or, as one translation renders it, ". . . making peace through the blood of his cross." This is not a peace made with God, but a God-made peace. The long struggle between the sin of man and the righteousness of God was brought to an honorable end in the cross of Christ; and now peace can be the portion of all who believe.

d. *Reconciliation.* "And you, that were sometime alienated and enemies in your mind by wicked works, yet now hath he reconciled in the body of his flesh through death, to present you holy and unblameable and unreproveable in his sight" (vv. 21, 22). The cross is such an overwhelming manifestation of God's holy love and justice that to get a true vision of it is to have the enmity of the heart slain, and to experience the reconciliation which follows through repentance toward God and faith in our Lord Jesus Christ.

2. Christ in us

"Christ in you, the hope of glory" (v. 27). Note also Galatians 2:20.

The convert must be taught something of

a. *The miracle of Christ's incoming.* Even though we speak so simply of receiving the Lord Jesus into our hearts and lives, we must never forget that His incoming constitutes one of the greatest mysteries and miracles in the universe. The Apostle Paul speaks of it as the secret which was hidden from angels and men in all ages, but now has been revealed to us (Ephesians 3:1-12).

It involves nothing less than

(1) *A miraculous operation.* Praying for the Ephesian believers, the great apostle says: "I bow my knees unto the Father of our Lord Jesus Christ . . . that he would grant you, according to the riches of his glory, to be strengthened with might by his Spirit in the inner man; that Christ may dwell in your hearts by faith" (Ephesians 3:14, 16, 17). This miraculous operation of the Holy Spirit is necessary, in order to strengthen our inner man to say yes to the incoming of Christ, and to enable us to stand the wonder of His indwelling.

(2) *A miraculous revelation.* It seems that Saul of Tarsus had two distinct revelations of the Lord Jesus at the time of his conversion. The first occurred when God revealed Jesus to him on the way to Damascus (Acts 9:3-5). This revelation slew the enmity of his heart and led him to surrender to Jesus as Saviour and Lord. The second revelation appears to have occurred while he was at prayer in Damascus, waiting for God's next step for his life.

The apostle later recalls this experience when he says, "It pleased God . . . to reveal his Son in me" (Galatians 1:15, 16). Such a revelation was not only miraculous; it was utterly transforming and compelling. Immediately following it, the young believer became convinced of God's power and purpose for his life, without having to solict advice or help from man.

How the soul-winner needs to bring home to the young convert the true meaning of Christ's indwelling!

b. *The measure of Christ's indwelling.* "The riches of the glory of this mystery . . . which is Christ in you" (Colossians 1:27). Notice also Paul's prayer for the Ephesian church: ". . . that Christ may dwell in your hearts by faith" (Ephesians 3:17).

Dr. Handley C. G. Moule, in his commentary on Ephesians, points out that the word "dwell" here means "settled residence" or "to be at home." So the apostle's longing for the saints at Ephesus was that Christ might be "at home" in their lives.

With many Christians there seems to be a very wide gap between the acceptance of Christ's incoming and the acknowledgment of Christ's indwelling. The convert must be taught from the very beginning to "sanctify the Lord God" in his heart (I Peter 3:15).

For Christ to be hallowed as Lord, He must be given the best room in the house, which is the heart; and complete Lordship throughout the home, which is the life. Only then can the believer truly say, "Christ liveth in me" (Galatians 2:20).

This is the *means* of achieving the goal of presenting every man perfect in Christ.

But next consider

II. THE METHOD OF ACHIEVING THIS TARGET

As soul-winners we are to "preach, warning every man, and teaching every man in all wisdom" (Colossians 1:28).

Two methods of instruction are set forth here:

1. Warning every man

This is the negative side. There are many things about which the convert should be warned. He must not be given the idea that, because he has trusted Christ, there is nothing more about which to be concerned; that all is well; that there are no more problems, difficulties, or trials ahead! On the contrary, he should be warned about

a. *The deceitfulness of sin.* See I John 1:6—2:2. John, that great undershepherd, is telling his converts here that if they say they have no sin, they deceive themselves and the truth is not in them.

The babe in Christ must be taught that full salvation should be considered in three aspects—salvation in the past, present, and future. The past deals with the penalty of sin; the present, with the power of sin; and the future, with the presence of sin.

In view of this, a person can be truly saved and yet be conscious of inward sin. On the other hand, while sin is dormant, it need not be dominant. (See Romans 6:12-14.)

Because it is dominant, however, it follows that, until the day of final deliverance, sin can defeat and defile; and for this reason there is need for confession and cleansing (see I John 1:9).

b. *The devices of Satan.* (See II Corinthians 2:11.) Until a person is converted, he may not be aware of Satan's presence and activity in the world; but this is completely changed, once a soul trusts the Saviour.

On this point the apostle could speak from firsthand experience, for he said, "We are not ignorant of his [the devil's] devices."

Thank God, however, there is victory for the feeblest Christian who knows how to submit himself to God and resist the devil. (See James 4:7 and Revelation 12:9-11.)

c. *The desires of self.* (See Galatians 5:16-26.) The newly committed Christian discovers not only the presence of sin and the power of Satan but also the problem of self—the old nature: for "the flesh lusteth against the Spirit, and the Spirit against the flesh: and these are contrary the one to the other" (Galatians 5:17).

Here again instruction must be given to starve the "old man" and feed the "new man." To fulfill this simple injunction in the power of the Holy Spirit is to know victory day by day. (See Romans 13:14; Galatians 5:25; Ephesians 4:22-24.)

2. Teaching every man

Jesus commissioned His apostles to make disciples by teaching them to observe all things whatsoever He had commanded them (Matthew 28:19, 20). So the convert must be taught to continue "stedfastly in the apostles' doctrine and fellowship, and in breaking of bread, and in prayers" (Acts 2:42).

Notice how Paul carried this out in his own ministry (Acts 20:27). Examine the amount of teaching contained in I and II Thessalonians, in the light of about three weeks' evangelistic campaign in that city!

So the soul-winner is to warn and teach his converts, in order to present them "perfect in Christ Jesus."

There is one other thought which deserves attention:

III. THE MANNER OF ACHIEVING THIS TARGET

"Whereunto I also labour," says Paul, "striving according to his working, which worketh in me mightily" (Colossians 1:29). From this and other similar verses throughout the apostle's writings, we learn that in order to achieve the goal of presenting every man perfect in Christ Jesus, the soul-winner must know something of

1. The concern of the father

". . . in Christ Jesus I have begotten you through the gospel" (I Corinthians 4:15). The great-hearted apostle here wishes to remind his readers of his own paternal rights, which could never be invalidated by subsequent laborers in the field. As a father, he had a real concern for his children, beseeching them to be followers of him (see I Corinthians 4:16).

2. The travail of the mother

"My little children, of whom I travail in birth again until Christ be formed in you" (Galatians 4:19). The parental relationship is expressed in tenderest form. Paul writes here not as a father but, rather, as a mother.

Jesus described this experience when He said, "A woman when she is in travail hath sorrow, because her hour is come: but as soon as she is delivered of the child, she remembereth no more the anguish, for joy that a man is born into the world" (John 16:21).

3. The sacrifice of the lover

"I will very gladly spend and be spent for you; though the more abundantly I love you, the less I be loved" (II Corinthians 12:15). As the lover of their souls, he was prepared to spare no labor, self-denial, or suffering, that he might woo them for his Master. And note carefully that this avowal of ever increasing and superabundant love for them is set over against the ever diminishing requital of it by his readers.

4. The jealousy of the friend

"I am jealous over you with a godly jealousy: for I have espoused you to one husband, that I may present you as a chaste virgin to Christ" (II Corinthians 11:2).

Here, of course, Paul speaks as the Bridegroom's friend, and expresses a holy jealousy and fear, lest by any means, "as the serpent beguiled Eve through his subtilty," so his converts "should be corrupted from the simplicity that is in Christ" (II Corinthians 11:3).

Like John the Baptist before him, Paul could anticipate no greater joy than that of presenting his converts to Christ as "a chaste virgin" (see John 3:29, 30).

5. The gentleness of the nurse

"We were gentle among you, even as a nurse cherisheth her children" (I Thessalonians 2:7-9). What love and experience —in delivering and developing a babe—are linked together in the twin thoughts of mother and nurse!

Most scholars see here the thought of the nursing mother, cherishing her children, being affectionately desirous that they should grow up to be healthy and strong.

6. The authority of the officer

"Thou therefore endure hardness, as a good soldier of Jesus Christ" (II Timothy 2:3, 4). As a good soldier himself, the apostle was here inviting his son in the faith to suffer affliction with him in the cause of the gospel. His desire for Timothy was that he should fight manfully under Christ's banner, against sin, the world, and the devil; and continue as a faithful soldier unto the end of life.

7. The striving of the servant

"I am made a minister . . . whereunto I also labour, striving. . . ." (Colossians 1:25-29).

As a minister, or servant of the Lord Jesus, the apostle exerted himself like an athlete, laboring and striving in order to present every man perfect in Christ. Both the words "labor" and "striving" are metaphors from the arena, and convey the idea of agony and exertion.

The soul-winner must be a believer of many parts if he is to achieve the goal of bringing his converts to perfection in Christ.

Sometimes he must be a father; at other times he must be a mother; and on occasions he must be a lover or a servant—until his task is complete.

God enable us to be soul-winners with the true target before us.

THE SOUL-WINNER'S TRAVAIL

Scriptures for Study

I say the truth in Christ, I lie not, my conscience also bearing me witness in the Holy Ghost,

That I have great heaviness and continual sorrow in my heart.

For I could wish that myself were accursed from Christ for my brethren, my kinsmen according to the flesh:

Who are Israelites; to whom pertaineth the adoption, and the glory, and the covenants, and the giving of the law, and the service of God, and the promises;

Whose are the fathers, and of whom as concerning the flesh Christ came, who is over all, God blessed for ever. Amen.

—ROMANS 9:1-5

Brethren, my heart's desire and prayer to God for Israel is, that they might be saved.

—ROMANS 10:1

Chapter 7

THE SOUL-WINNER'S TRAVAIL

WRITING TO THE THESSALONIANS and recalling his soul-winning work among them, the Apostle Paul says: "Remember . . . our labour and travail . . . because . . . we preached unto you the gospel" (I Thessalonians 2:9).

The expression "travail" here denotes the toil, labor, and weariness which were involved in bringing those men and women at Thessalonica to a personal knowledge of Christ. Souls are not easily won, although they may appear to be when we observe the glamorized mass evangelism of a modern age. Men and women can never be born into the kingdom of God without tears and travail. Even if an evangelist does not pay the price, God has His own who are prepared to suffer with Christ in order to bring to birth His redemptive purposes in the world.

When Paul says: "My little children, of whom I travail in birth again until Christ be formed in you . . ." he is obviously referring to the initial travail which he must have experienced when he brought into being, under God, the church at Galatia, as well as to his subsequent travail as he saw these Galatian Christians lapse into legalism. (See Galatians 4:19.)

What this soul travail involves is best summed up for us in the opening verses of Romans 9. It is not without significance that this passage follows hard upon chapter 8 of Romans; for only a man who knows the Spirit-filled life of Romans 8 can appreciate the evangelistic heartthrob of Romans 9.

From the divine standpoint, this section of the Epistle to
the Romans reveals how God, in sovereign righteousness, re-
lates His purposes of grace to His ancient people, the Jews.
From the believer's point of view, however, the verses before
us set forth the nature of a true passion for souls; and particularly how this passion expresses itself toward our own kith
and kin.

Let us, therefore, examine these words, with a prayer that
God will show us the passion which issues in the travail of
bringing souls to birth.

Notice, first of all, how Paul speaks of

I. A REAL PASSION FOR SOULS

"I say the truth in Christ, I lie not, my conscience also bearing me witness in the Holy Ghost" (Romans 9:1).

In these words, the spring of a real passion for souls is
traced to

1. A true experience of Christ

"I say the truth in Christ, I lie not." Weymouth renders this,
"I am telling you the truth as a Christian." The thought here
is that an experience of Christ is inseparably associated with
a passion for souls. In other words, no one can be a real
Christian without sharing something of the Saviour's travail
for the lost. To say that unconverted people around us do not
concern us, is to reveal that our Christianity is nothing more
than head knowledge, which puffs up into proud orthodoxy.
If and when a so-called Christian reaches this state of mind,
he becomes like the scribes and Pharisees of whom Jesus had
to say, "Ye compass sea and land to make one proselyte, and
when he is made, ye make him twofold more the child of hell
than yourselves" (Matthew 23:15). There is all the difference in the world between evangelizing and proselytizing.

A true experience of Christ leads to

2. A true exercise of conscience

". . . my conscience also bearing me witness in the Holy Ghost." Intimate fellowship with the Lord Jesus is always followed by an exercise of conscience regarding the lost. The Holy Spirit sees to it that the heartthrobs of the Saviour for men and women are made real in the believer's conscience. The Holy Spirit witnesses to our spirits concerning what is going on in the heart of Christ. We need to ask ourselves why we often have a conscience about jealousy, pride, thieving, swearing, and the like; but fail to have any exercise of conscience concerning our fellow men who are going to hell. The obvious answer is that our fellowship with Christ is not close enough to cause us to sense or hear the Holy Spirit's witness to our own conscience. Our constant prayer to God should be that He would give us such a true experience of Christ that our conscience may be ever sensitive to the needs of the lost.

Paul's words reveal not only a real passion for souls but also

II. A REGULAR PASSION FOR SOULS

"I have great heaviness and continual sorrow in my heart" (Romans 9:2).

It is clear that the apostle's passion for souls was nothing spasmodic or intermittent. His experience was rather one of continual heaviness and anguish of heart on behalf of the lost.

Consider for a moment the significance of these two statements:

1. Continual heaviness

This great soul-winner calls it "great heaviness," indicating that every day the weight of concern grew heavier and heavier. Which of us can dare to face this testimony of Paul without a sense of guilt? Often our experience is just the opposite. In the glow of our first love we were eager to win the lost:

we prayed; we watched; we sought. But as the days have passed, so the weight of that early concern has lifted, until now we are careless and sometimes lighthearted about the whole matter. We find it much easier to escape into administrative and organizational aspects of the work of God. We become absorbed with things, instead of being concerned for men and women. God have mercy upon us!

Such was the pressure on the spirit of God's servant that it led from continual heaviness to

2. Continual heartbreak

"I have . . . sorrow in my heart." Sheer heaviness of spirit brought him to tears: yes, real tears; not crocodile tears. On another occasion he could remind his brethren that "by the space of three years" he "ceased not to warn every one night and day with tears" (Acts 20:31).

And Paul was not the only man who wept for souls. There was the Master Himself, who stands alone in His continual sorrow and anguish of heart for souls. We read that He was a Man of "strong crying and tears" (Hebrews 5:7). He was a Man of "sorrows, and acquainted with grief" (Isaiah 53:3).

From the Gospels we learn that He wept over individuals. At Lazarus' grave, He "groaned in the spirit, and was troubled. . . . Jesus wept" (John 11:33-35). We do not believe He wept because of Lazarus' death. As the omniscient One, He knew that His friend was now free from sin and suffering; and in the highest interests, He could not wish him back. It is true that His sympathetic heart must have shared the sorrow of Martha and Mary. But we are not satisfied to think that this was why He troubled His spirit, groaned, and wept. We are more disposed to believe that His loving heart yearned and travailed for the hypocritically religious, self-righteous individuals who stood around that grave.

Then there were occasions when He wept over crowds.

Mark tells us that "Jesus, when he came out, saw much people, and was moved with compassion toward them, because they were as sheep not having a shepherd" (Mark 6:34; see also Matthew 9:36; 14:14).

That word "compassion" is one which people do not like to examine etymologically. They would say that it is bad taste. But Matthew and Mark knew what it meant when they first wrote it. It conveys the idea of yearning. The Greeks held the view that all emotion was centered in the bowels, so that to be deeply concerned and moved was to have "the bowels of compassion." It denotes the inward pain and yearning which a mother experiences over her wandering boy. Are we moved in this fashion, as we look upon the multitudes who surge down the streets of our modern towns and cities, as sheep having no shepherd?

Jesus also wept over cities. Think of the occasion when He cried: "O Jerusalem, Jerusalem, thou that killest the prophets, and stonest them which are sent unto thee, how often would I have gathered thy children together, even as a hen gathereth her chickens under her wings, and ye would not! Behold, your house is left unto you desolate" (Matthew 23:37, 38).

The thought that this great, proud, religious city had not discerned the day of her visitation, and was about to reject and crucify her Messiah, broke the Saviour's heart. He who could have sent legions of angels to slaughter man and beast, and raze to the ground the stately buildings, wept instead over a lost city.

History is replete with illustrations of genuine soul-winners, who have shared this same passion. After all, if anyone can say, "I live; yet not I, but Christ liveth in me," surely his outward manifestation of concern should witness to the compassionate Christ who dwells within.

Robert Murray McCheyne was one such man. His tears

and travail for souls are still spoken of in Scotland, even though he died more than a generation ago.

General Booth wept his way into human hearts. On one occasion, when a young Salvation Army captain wrote him, saying that he did not seem to evoke any response from the people under his charge, the General replied by a telegram bearing two words, "Try tears."

The psalmist was well acquainted with the principle of fruit out of travail when he wrote, "They that sow in tears shall reap in joy" (Psalm 126:5).

It is well to challenge our hearts as to whether or not we know anything of such travail and tears for souls. How many times have we asked God to put our "tears into" His "bottle" (Psalm 56:8), knowing that such weeping has represented, not sorrow for backsliding, not sorrow for our own sin, but a heartbreaking concern for men and women out of Christ?

The apostle shows us here that his concern for his brethren and kinsmen in the flesh was not only real and regular but also

III. A REDEMPTIVE PASSION FOR SOULS

"For I could wish that myself were accursed from Christ for my brethren, my kinsmen according to the flesh" (Romans 9:3).

This is where we begin to flounder. The words of truth and experience find their deepest level here. In our attempt to try to expound this statement, we find our key in the word "redemptive." We are told to redeem "the time, because the days are evil" (Ephesians 5:16), by which the apostle means working out in our everyday lives the triumph of the redemptive act of Christ at Calvary.

So a redemptive passion is oneness with Christ in the fellowship of His sufferings (see Philippians 3:10). This fellowship is not suffering for sin, which deserves punishment; nor is it so much suffering in service, which costs persecution. It is sharing in the outworking of God's purpose in redemption in the winning of souls; and this means passion.

It is only such a redemptive passion which

1. Adopts the shame of winning the lost

Paul refers to his nation as "my brethren, my kinsmen." He was prepared to identify himself with those he was trying to win. While he recognized that, as a nation, they had been favored with unique privileges and glory, he had to share the shame that they were now

a. *Blind.* "Blindness in part is happened to Israel" (Romans 11:25). O the shame of it! Once these people were the recipients of divine glory, the covenants, the giving of the law, the service of God, and the promises; but now they were spiritually blind.

b. *Boastful.* "Going about to establish their own righteousness," they had "not submitted themselves unto the righteousness of God" (Romans 10:3). Paul accepts the shame of this pride, arrogance, and hardness of heart as if it were his very own.

c. *Bitter.* Looking back into history, the apostle quotes Elijah, saying: "They have killed thy prophets, and digged down thine altars" (Romans 11:3; compare I Kings 19:10, 14). Paul's own experience shows how they had despised him, beaten him, stoned him, and attempted to take his life. But such was his redemptive concern for his brethren and kinsmen that he was prepared to adopt their shame. He was willing to become "as a Jew" in order that he might win "the Jews" (I Corinthians 9:20).

This redemptive passion goes further, however.   It

2. Accepts the sacrifice of winning the lost

"I could wish . . . myself . . . accursed from Christ" (Romans 9:3). This is beyond us. We cannot understand it. All we can say is that Paul was prepared to go to hell, if by that means his kinsmen in the flesh could be saved. Such a desire could never be fulfilled, because it would involve robbery of himself from the Lord who bought him; and having been redeemed, he could not be lost (John 10:28-30). Yet Paul was quite sober in making that statement. In fact, he was speaking by inspiration of the Holy Spirit. We can only conclude, therefore, that Paul intended to convey the extraordinary reaches of sacrifice to which he was prepared to go.

For the Saviour, this redemptive concern meant the tasting of death for every man (Hebrews 2:9). Thank God, such a tasting of death has never to be repeated! This is the aspect of the redemptive work of Christ in which no one can share. And yet—let us make no mistake about it—there is an *outworking* of that redemptive suffering in which the believer can participate. Indeed, without fellowship with Christ on this level, we can never become the effective soul-winners God has intended us to be. Paul speaks of this suffering as filling up "that which is behind of the afflictions of Christ" (Colossians 1:24).

Dr. J. H. Jowett reminds us that "the gospel of a broken heart begins with the ministry of bleeding hearts." And again, "As soon as we cease to bleed, we cease to bless." We must bleed if we would be ministers of the saving blood.

When Charles Peace, that notorious murderer, saw for the first time the significance of the cross of Christ, he said that he would be willing to walk from the north to the south of the British Isles barefooted on broken glass, to tell the story of Christ's power to save!

General Booth once said that he would like to send all his

candidates for officership to hell for twenty-four hours, as the chief part of their training. Only thus would they be able to accept the sacrifice of winning the lost.

Out of the sacrifice of winning the lost, however, we notice that a redemptive passion triumphantly

3. Anticipates the satisfaction of winning the lost

Later, continuing this same subject, the Apostle Paul says, "My heart's desire and prayer to God for Israel is that they might be saved" (Romans 10:1). To carry through this work of redemption, our Lord "endured the cross, depising the shame" for "the joy that was set before him" (Hebrews 12:2). It was the joy not only of doing the will of God but of "bringing many sons unto glory" (Hebrews 2:10). This is the crown of rejoicing for every true soul-winner. This is the promised resurrection from the depths of shame and sacrifice into which the soul-winner has to plunge himself, in his search for sinners away from God. No wonder the soul-winner's joy will be full when he stands before his Lord in the glory-land with those he has won to the Master through his faithful witness.

What a ministry, then, is this redemptive passion! Do you know anything about it in your life? Or is this language strange and unintelligible? Do you know what it is to suffer with Christ?

This concern for the lost is not a matter of emotional stirrings. It is the work of the Holy Spirit in our hearts, as we deliberately accept this fellowship of suffering and, through ever increasing fellowship with Christ, learn something of the meaning of His cross, the value He sets on the human soul, the eternal doom of the lost which He has disclosed, the nearness of His return which He has foretold, and the inestimable loss or gain at His judgment seat which He has declared awaits the believer.

It is only when we are willing to pay the price of this soul-saving ministry that we can honestly pray those solemn words of Amy Wilson Carmichael:

> O for a passionate passion for souls;
> O for a pity that yearns;
> O for a love that loves unto death;
> O for a heart that burns!

THE SOUL-WINNER'S TRIALS

Scriptures for Study

For though I be free from all men, yet have I made myself servant unto all, that I might gain the more.

And unto the Jews I became as a Jew, that I might gain the Jews; to them that are under the law, as under the law, that I might gain them that are under the law;

To them that are without law, as without law, (being not without law to God, but under the law to Christ,) that I might gain them that are without law.

—I Corinthians 9:19-21

He that descended is the same also that ascended up far above all heavens, that he might fill all things.

And he gave some, apostles; and some, prophets; and some, evangelists; and some, pastors and teachers;

For the perfecting of the saints, for the work of the ministry, for the edifying of the body of Christ:

Till we all come in the unity of the faith, and of the knowledge of the Son of God, unto a perfect man, unto the measure of the stature of the fulness of Christ:

That we henceforth be no more children, tossed to and fro, and carried about with every wind of doctrine, by the sleight of men, and cunning craftiness, whereby they lie in wait to deceive.

—Ephesians 4:10-14

For when for the time ye ought to be teachers, ye have need that one teach you again which be the first principles of the oracles of God; and are become such as have need of milk, and not of strong meat.

For every one that useth milk is unskillful in the word of righteousness: for he is a babe.

But strong meat belongeth to them that are of full age, even those who by reason of use have their senses exercised to discern both good and evil.

—HEBREWS 5:12-14

And I, brethren, could not speak unto you as unto spiritual, but as unto carnal, even as unto babes in Christ.

I have fed you with milk, and not with meat: for hitherto ye were not able to bear it, neither yet now are ye able.

For ye are yet carnal: for whereas there is among you envying, and strife, and divisions, are ye not carnal, and walk as men?

For while one saith, I am of Paul; and another, I am of Apollos; are ye not carnal?

Who then is Paul, and who is Apollos, but ministers by whom ye believed, even as the Lord gave to every man?

I have planted, Apollos watered; but God gave the increase.

—I CORINTHIANS 3:1-6

Obey them that have the rule over you, and submit yourselves: for they watch for your souls, as they that must give account, that they may do it with joy, and not with grief: for that is unprofitable for you.

—HEBREWS 13:17

Chapter 8

THE SOUL-WINNER'S TRIALS

THE STUDY OF THE SCRIPTURES, coupled with experience in evangelism, teaches us that the trials of the soul-winner cover three stages of the convert's life.

I. THE TRIALS OF WINNING THE CONVERT

In his endeavor to win men and women to Christ, the Apostle Paul says: "I am made all things to all men, that I might by all means save some" (I Corinthians 9:22).

If you look carefully at the context, you will observe that the writer refers to four classes of people of comprehensive significance, whom he was seeking to influence for Christ:

1. The religionists—the Jews

"And unto the Jews I became as a Jew, that I might gain the Jews" (I Corinthians 9:20).

An illustration of this is provided for us in Acts 16:1-3. Paul had gone to Lystra and had met there a certain disciple named Timotheus, whose mother was a Jewess and whose father was a Greek. And we read: "Him would Paul have to go forth with him; and took and circumcised him because of the Jews which were in those quarters: for they knew all that his father was a Greek." Here Paul was behaving as a Jew, in order to win the Jews.

2. The moralists—those under the law

"To them that are under the law, as under the law" (I Corinthians 9:20).

An illustration of this is provided for us in Acts 21:17-26. Paul was in Jerusalem and was reporting on all that God was doing in and through him, by the preaching of the free grace of God. But lest his approach should offend the moralists, he submitted to certain legal and ceremonial rites, in order that he might win them that were under the law. His Jewish brethren advised him to submit to the law of purifying, adding, ". . . that . . . all may know . . . that thou thyself also walkest orderly, and keepest the law." The record goes on to say: "Paul took the men . . . the next day purifying himself with them."

3. The worldings—those without the law

"To them that are without law, as without law (being not without law to God, but under the law to Christ), that I might gain them that are without law" (I Corinthians 9:21).

An illustration of this is provided for us in Acts 17:16-34. This time Paul was in the heathen city of Athens, and his spirit was stirred within him because he saw the people wholly given over to idolatry. When provided with an opportunity to preach to the great masses of the city, he took full advantage of it and his entire approach was one which would appeal to those without the law. He even quoted from their own poets, in order to gain their ear (see verses 28, 29).

4. The moral weaklings—"the weak"

"To the weak became I as weak, that I might gain the weak" (I Corinthians 9:22).

An illustration of this is provided for us in I Corinthians 8:9-13. It is true that Paul was here addressing believers who were weak in faith, but the passage none the less gives us an insight into Paul's carefulness in becoming all things to all men, that he might win some. His principle was that he would by no means use his liberty (power) in the gospel, so as to become "a stumbling block to them that are weak."

In our attempt to win people in each of these categories, we may meet with four types of trial:

1. Furious resistance

Stephen was confronted with such resistance and had to declare: "Ye stiffnecked and uncircumcised in heart and ears, ye do always resist the Holy Ghost: as your fathers did, so do ye."

And such was the fury and hatred in their hearts that ". . . when they heard these things, they were cut to the heart, and they gnashed on him with their teeth . . . and cast him out of the city, and stoned him" (Acts 7:51, 54, 58).

There are times when the soul-winner has to face all kinds of situations. The Lord Jesus forewarned that it would be so, and we must not be surprised if we meet such furious resistance. (See John 15:18-23; 16:1, 2.)

2. Spurious acceptance

Luke tells a sad story of a certain man called Simon, of the city of Samaria, who was a sorcerer. When the gospel was preached, he gave heed and apparently believed, was baptized, and continued with Philip, the evangelist. But his profession of faith was spurious. Deep down in his heart he had not believed on the Lord Jesus Christ. He was only desirous of possessing the strange, miraculous power which he saw demonstrated by the apostles. His motive was entirely wrong. Peter detected this and, addressing him, said, "Thy money perish with thee, because thou hast thought that the gift of God may be purchased with money. Thou hast neither part nor lot in this matter: for thy heart is not right in the sight of

God. Repent therefore of this thy wickedness, and pray God, if perhaps the thought of thine heart may be forgiven thee. For I perceive that thou art in the gall of bitterness, and in the bond of iniquity" (Acts 8:20-23; compare vv. 9-24).

3. Curious indifference

As Paul was preaching at Athens, "when they heard of the resurrection of the dead, some mocked" (Acts 17:32). Until time is no more, there always will be the mockers who, with an air of indifference, laugh at matters of eternal consequence.

The same attitude of curious indifference is exemplified in another mood by Gallio, who, when face to face with spiritual issues, is reported to have "cared for none of those things" (Acts 18:17).

4. Serious reluctance

In the same crowd at Athens were not only those who mocked but others who said: "We will hear thee again of this matter" (Acts 17:32). They procrastinated.

Another instance of this serious reluctance is illustrated in the case of Felix, who, having heard Paul preach in power of "righteousness, temperance, and judgment to come," trembled with fear; but when challenged to make some decision, answered: "Go thy way for this time; when I have a convenient season, I will call for thee" (Acts 24:25).

Here, then, are some of the trials of winning the convert. Thank God, in spite of furious resistance, spurious acceptance, curious indifference, and serious reluctance, there are those who truly believe!

Even in Athens, after being mocked and set aside by some, Paul led others to Christ; for "certain men clave unto him, and believed." Among these were certain notables like "Dionysius the Areopagite, and a woman named Damaris, and others with them" (Acts 17:34).

The seed of the gospel may fall by the wayside, on stony ground, or among thorns; but there is always some which falls on the good soil and springs up into "fruit," "more fruit," and "much fruit." So along with the trials of winning the convert, there are also the triumphs.

The second stage of soul-winning involves the soul-winner in

II. THE TRIALS OF WEANING THE CONVERT

Paul's sorrow and trial, when writing to the believers at Corinth, was that he could not address them as mature Christians, even after a long period of time. They were still unweaned babes. Perhaps this is one of the most common trials of the soul-winner.

From the Word of God we learn that there are certain evidences that a babe in Christ has not been weaned. There is

1. Unstableness in the Christian life

Observe how this is described in Paul's exhortation to the Ephesian Christians: ". . . that we henceforth be no more children, tossed to and fro, and carried about with every wind of doctrine, by the sleight of men, and cunning craftiness, whereby they lie in wait to deceive" (Ephesians 4:14).

Unstableness in the Christian life means

a. *Being easily shifted,* "tossed to and fro, and carried about with every wind of doctrine." The metaphor employed here is that of a ship tossed by the waves and carried hither and thither by every windy blast. It is descriptive of the changing thoughts, tempers, and tastes of spiritual childishness!

With characteristic unstableness, such babes in the Christian life establish so-called convictions at one moment, only to contradict them at a later moment. They never can speak with authority or confidence. Tossed to and fro, they are like mariners aboard a ship without compass, chart, or rudder.

b. *Being easily seduced,* "carried . . . by the sleight of men, and cunning craftiness. . . ." This indicates that there are two ways in which unstable Christians are led astray:

(1) *Religious cleverness,* "the sleight of men." The term denotes the quickness, suddenness, and deceitfulness of the dice thrower. It is a warning against anything religious which is clever without being clear. Childlike, the unstable Christian will often be impressed and seduced by that which appeals to the senses only. How the convert needs to be warned of the tricks, stunts, and magic of certain religious cults and movements today!

(2) *Religious craftiness,* "cunning craftiness." From the construction of this phrase it seems quite clear that Paul had in mind the deeper and more subtle forms of delusion. In all probability, "cunning craftiness" was the particular scheme of erroneous teaching which had already struck root in the soil of Asia Minor.

Such craftiness, devoted to the systematic plan of deceit in innumerable forms, is still with us today. Think, for instance, of such deceptive systems as Romanism, Spiritism, Modernism, twentieth century Judaism, Russellism, Christadelphianism, Unitarianism, British Israelism, and the like.

2. Unskillfulness in the Christian life

The writer to the Hebrews sums it up when he says, "Every one that useth milk is unskillful in the word of righteousness: for he is a babe" (Hebrews 5:13).

These words were addressed to those who had lost interest in the deeper truths of Christianity and were making the milk of the Word their only diet. Being mostly Jews, they were still in bondage to the ritual and traditions of their childhood days. How true this is of so many today! Saved for years, but still drinking milk; still wrapped up in the baby garments of their first days in Christ!

Such unskillfulness in the Christian life involves

a. *Failure to rightly appreciate the truth.* The senses are not "exercised to discern both good and evil" (Hebrews 5:14). The popular milk-and-water ministry may be desired and enjoyed; but when it comes to pure, rich milk, or the meat of the Word, it is not appreciated. Through lack of growth and experience in the Word of righteousness, the babe in Christ has no discernment of truth.

b. *Failure to rightly apply the truth.* "For every one that useth milk is unskillful in the word of righteousness" (Hebrews 5:13). "The word of righteousness" must signify fully developed Christian teaching. By being "unskillful in the word of righteousness," the writer implies the inexperienced handling and applying of God's Word; or the very antithesis of that relevant injunction in II Timothy 2:15, "Study to show thyself approved unto God, a workman that needeth not to be ashamed, rightly dividing the word of truth."

3. Unspirituality in the Christian life

In that classic word picture of spiritual babyhood, recorded in I Corinthians 3, Paul tells us that the believer who never seems to pass the baby stage is unspiritual. Listen to his words, "And I, brethren, could not speak unto you as unto spiritual, but as unto carnal [unspiritual], even as unto babes in Christ. . . . For ye are yet carnal [unspiritual]: for whereas there is among you envying, and strife, and divisions, are ye not carnal [unspiritual], and walk as men?" (vv. 1-3).

Such unspirituality is marked by

a. *Unhealthy discontent.* "There is among you envying." How accurate Paul is! For we all know how discontented and envious a child becomes when he ceases to be the center of attraction and the object of interest. In a similar way, these Corinthian babes had become discontented through being envious of one another's hero speakers, since such hero worship served to draw attention to themselves. To them, the message which the apostles preached was secondary: what really mattered was whether or not they themselves belonged to a prominent section of the Church. What unspirituality!

b. *Unhealthy discord.* "There is among you . . . strife." Watch a nursery of discontented babes, and it will not be long before you see discord and strife. The same is true in the Church. Where there are those who refuse to grow up, one often finds discord and strife. Everything that happens and everyone who ministers become bones of contention.

c. *Unhealthy division.* "There is among you . . . divisions." So the Apostle Paul speaks of the factions or cliques which these Christian babes had created. Instead of finding their center in Christ, they were saying: "I am of Paul"; "I am of Apollos"; "I am of Cephas"; "I am of Christ." Think of it! Bringing Christ down to the level of others, instead of making Him the one and only Center of all true fellowship! Denominationalism and sectarianism are nothing new. Whether in Paul's day or in our day, they are a sure mark of spiritual babyhood. How repelling are these characteristics of unspirituality; and yet how often they are seen in the lives of our converts! The soul-winner's task must be to travail again and again in prayer and instruction, until the babes in Christ are weaned from these associations of spiritual childishness. The servant of God will find it a costly business; many trials will beset his way; but how worthwile to present every man perfect in Christ!

Even after the weaning of the convert, however, there are

III. THE TRIALS OF WATCHING THE CONVERT

Although the words of Hebrews 13:17, "them that have the rule over you [or, guide you]," refer primarily to the leaders in the Church, doubtless soul-winners are included when the writer exhorts the believers to "obey them," adding, "They watch for your souls, as they that must give account, that they may do it with joy, and not with grief: for that is unprofitable for you."

The trials of watching our converts include seeing them at times

1. Backslide through disobedience

Writing to the believers at Galatia, Paul the apostle had to ask them: "Ye did run well; who did hinder you [drive you back] that ye should not obey the truth?" (Galatians 5:7). Progress in the Christian life is dependent upon obedience to revealed truth. If and when the convert fails to obey any given truth, then there is backsliding.

The life of liberty through the power of the Spirit had been clearly presented to these Galatian believers, but in spite of this they had allowed the Judaizers with their teaching to drive them back into disobedience. Instead of standing fast in the liberty wherewith Christ had made them free, they had become entangled again with the yoke of bondage.

How true is the little chorus:

> Trust and obey,
> For there's no other way
> To be happy in Jesus
> But to trust and obey!

2. Backslide through drifting

Addressing Jewish Christians who were in danger of backsliding because of enemy pressure, the writer to the Hebrews

says, "Therefore we ought to give the more earnest heed to
the things which we have heard, lest at any time we should
let them slip [or, more literally, drift away]" (Hebrews 2:1).
Through inattention and indiscipline in matters spiritual, it is
easy for Christians, young or old, to drift away—first imper-
ceptibly, but sooner or later indisputably. How the soul-
winner needs to watch his children in the faith, lest under his
very eyes they drift away from the things which they have
heard!

3. Backslide through discouragement

Later on in the same Epistle to the Hebrews, the Spirit of
God exhorts all Christian people, saying: "Consider him that
endured such contradiction of sinners against himself, lest ye
be wearied and faint in your minds" (Hebrews 12:3; compare
vv. 1-4). Nothing leads to spiritual discouragement like the
weariness and faintheartedness which come through "the
contradiction of sinners." Our archenemy, Satan, has a very
subtle and effective way of wearing down the young convert
by various forms of contradiction. The Lord Jesus summed
it up when He talked about men who say all manner of evil
against us falsely for His sake (Matthew 5:11).

If the soul-winner is watching carefully, he will detect the
disobedience, and counter it by stimulating new love and
loyalty to Christ. He will notice the drifting, and bring home
to the young believer the solemn consequences of a life of
indiscipline and ineffectiveness. He will observe when the
spirit of discouragement is attacking the newly committed
Christian and will turn his eyes unto Jesus; for it is only as
we "consider him" that we shall be saved from being "wearied and faint" in our minds. "Looking off to Jesus" is the
secret of rising above fears, failures, and frustrations.

These are some of the trials which the soul-winner is bound
to encounter in his high and holy task of winning men and

women to the Lord Jesus Christ. However, they are to be faced and fought if the Saviour's commission—to make disciples of all nations—is to be fulfilled. Our encouragement must ever be the knowledge that His Presence will be with us always, and the power of His Holy Spirit will enable us, even unto the consummation of the age.

THE SOUL-WINNER'S TEMPTATIONS

Scriptures for Study

Jesus saith unto them, My meat is to do the will of him that sent me, and to finish his work.

Say not ye, There are yet four months, and then cometh harvest? behold, I say unto you, Lift up your eyes, and look on the fields; for they are white already to harvest.
—JOHN 4:34, 35

My brethren, have not the faith of our Lord Jesus Christ, the Lord of glory, with respect of persons.

For if there come unto your assembly a man with a gold ring, in goodly apparel, and there come in also a poor man in vile raiment;

And ye have respect to him that weareth the gay clothing, and say unto him, Sit thou here in a good place; and say to the poor, Stand thou there, or sit here under my footstool:

Are ye not then partial in yourselves, and are become judges of evil thoughts?

Hearken, my beloved brethren, Hath not God chosen the poor of this world rich in faith, and heirs of the kingdom which he hath promised to them that love him?

But ye have despised the poor. Do not rich men oppress you, and draw you before the judgment seats?

Do not they blaspheme that worthy name by the which ye are called?

If ye fulfill the royal law according to the scripture, Thou shalt love thy neighbour as thyself, ye do well:

But if ye have respect to persons, ye commit sin, and are convinced of the law as transgressors.
—JAMES 2:1-9

For though I be free from all men, yet have I made my-self servant unto all, that I might gain the more.

And unto the Jews I became as a Jew, that I might gain the Jews; to them that are under the law, as under the law, that I might gain them that are under the law;

To them that are without law, as without law, (being not without law to God, but under the law to Christ,) that I might gain them that are without law.

To the weak became I as weak, that I might gain the weak: I am made all things to all men, that I might by all means save some.

And this I do for the gospel's sake, that I might be par-taker thereof with you.

Know ye not that they which run in a race run all, but one receiveth the prize? So run, that ye may obtain.

And every man that striveth for the mastery is temperate in all things. Now they do it to obtain a corruptible crown; but we an incorruptible.

I therefore so run, not as uncertainly; so fight I, not as one that beateth the air;

But I keep under my body, and bring it into subjection: lest that by any means, when I have preached to others, I myself should be a castaway.

—I CORINTHIANS 9:19-27

This is the will of God, even your sanctification, that ye should abstain from fornication:

That every one of you should know how to possess his vessel in sanctification and honour;

Not in the lust of concupiscence, even as the Gentiles which know not God:

That no man go beyond and defraud his brother in any matter: because that the Lord is the avenger of all such, as we also have forewarned you and testified.

—I THESSALONIANS 4:3-6

Chapter 9

THE SOUL-WINNER'S TEMPTATIONS

THE WORD OF GOD makes it plain that the temptations of the soul-winner can be spiritual, social, or sexual. In each of these realms temptation can be intensely real, and it behooves us to examine the approaches along which it can come, so as to be prepared for adequate resistance and victory. For the soul-winner to be forewarned in this respect is to be forearmed.

Let us, then, consider

I. THE SPIRITUAL TEMPTATIONS OF THE SOUL-WINNER

While temptations in the spiritual realm are many and varied, they are doubtless included in the four means which the enemy has chosen to use against the soul-winner.

1. Spiritual carelessness

Solomon's words in Proverbs 29:18 express a solemn principle: "Where there is no vision, the people perish." No passion for lost souls is the consequence of no vision. Jeremiah says: "Mine eye affecteth mine heart" (Lamentations 3:51).

We see how this is illustrated in the case of the disciples, when our Lord introduced them to the need of Samaria. Because their eyes were blind to the fields white unto harvest, their hearts were unaffected. Indeed, they marveled that the Master should talk to a woman who was a Samaritan. The fact that she was bound in sin, needing liberation, did not occur to them.

What the Saviour saw certainly affected His heart. He could say, "My meat is to do the will of him that sent me, and to finish his work. Say not ye, There are yet four months, and then cometh harvest? behold I say unto you, Lift up your eyes, and look on the fields; for they are white already to harvest" (John 4:34, 35).

How easy it is to be affected by spiritual carelessness! It is a temptation we must watch carefully.

2. Spiritual prayerlessness

Where there is carelessness, there follows prayerlessness; and Jesus said, "Men ought always to pray, and not to faint" (Luke 18:1).

Where there is no passion for souls, there is no prayer. The Lord Jesus clearly taught this when He said, "The harvest truly is plenteous, but the labourers are few; pray ye therefore the Lord of the harvest, that he will send forth labourers into his harvest" (Matthew 9:37, 38).

Even as He uttered these words, He "was moved with compassion . . . when he saw the multitudes . . . because they fainted, and were scattered abroad, as sheep having no shepherd" (v. 36).

When the Apostle Paul expresses his concern for his kindred according to the flesh (Romans 9:1-5), he continues, saying, "Brethren, my heart's desire and prayer to God for Israel is that they might be saved" (Romans 10:1).

When we yield to the temptation of prayerlessness, this is a sure evidence that we have lost the vision and passion for souls.

3. Spiritual fearfulness

As carelessness leads to prayerlessness, so prayerlessness leads to fearfulness. It was when the disciples were too weak and wayward to pray that they hid themselves behind closed doors "for fear of the Jews" (John 20:19). Well does Solomon say, "The fear of man bringeth a snare" (Proverbs 29:25).

Perhaps this fearfulness to open our mouths in confession of our faith or to take advantage of God-given opportunities for soul-winning is one of the most familiar and effective temptations of the enemy. Only the fullness and anointing of the Holy Spirit for service can overcome this paralyzing fear.

4. Spiritual weariness

Laboring against fear weakens the soul-winner. It was in the knowledge of this fact that the Apostle Paul wrote to the Galatian believers, saying, "Let us not be weary in well doing: for in due season we shall reap, if we faint not" (Galatians 6:9).

The same thought, in another context, occurs in Hebrews 12:3-4. "Consider him that endured such contradiction of sinners against himself, lest ye be wearied and faint in your minds. Ye have not yet resisted unto blood, striving against sin."

This spiritual weariness is not so much physical or mental tiredness in the work of God as a weariness of it. Literally, it means "to be beaten out," and leads to giving up or failing in duty.

Though these spiritual temptations are linked together, it is possible for the soul-winner to be attacked by them singly or jointly.

With the spiritual temptations, we must also think of

II. THE SOCIAL TEMPTATIONS OF THE SOUL-WINNER

The social temptations have mainly to do with the soul-winner's reactions to

1. Social distinctions

It is perilously possible for a genuine lover of souls to be affected by social distinctions in his work of winning men and women to Christ. By social distinctions we mean such differences as may be created by

a. *Race and religion.* The Apostle Paul, as a true evangelist, faced this problem, and could say, "I am debtor both to the Greeks, and to the Barbarians; both to the wise, and to the unwise. . . . For I am not ashamed of the gospel of Christ: for it is the power of God unto salvation to every one that believeth; to the Jew first, and also to the Greek" (Romans 1:14, 16).

Notice that Paul mentions the Greeks, who were the cultured people, with the classical civilization; the Barbarians, that is, the people of all the other nations; the wise, the intellectual people; the unwise, the simple people; the Jews, the religious people. These man-made distinctions made no difference to his sense of indebtedness to preach the gospel. He recognized that "there is no respect of persons with God" (Romans 2:11).

Peter had to learn this lesson before God could use him. At one time he was such a prejudiced Jew that on no account would he entertain the thought of preaching the gospel to the Gentiles. God had to give him a vision in which he saw all manner of four-footed beasts of the earth, wild beasts, creeping things, and fowls of the air, mingled together; and the command was, "Rise, Peter; kill, and eat." But Peter said, "Not so, Lord; for I have never eaten anything that is common or unclean." Then we read that "the voice spake unto him again the second time, What God hath cleansed, that call not thou common." (See Acts 10:11-16.) Immediately following this vision came an urgent appeal for spiritual help from the Gentile Cornelius, and Peter realized that this was a call from God. When he arrived at the house of Cornelius, he opened his mouth and said, "Of a truth I perceive that God is no respecter of persons" (Acts 10:34).

It is sad and serious to see how social distinctions still affect so-called Christian workers today. Race and religion still influence the appeal and approach of those who claim to be lovers of souls.

b. *Rank and riches.* Social distinctions arise, not only from the differences of race and religion, but also from the differences created by rank and riches. Perhaps this is one of the greatest curses of this age of materialism.

Even in the days of the Apostle James, this was a problem to be reckoned with. See what he has to say in James 2:1-9. There were high-minded people in the Church who would say to those who wore gay clothing, "Sit thou here in a good place"; and whisper to the poor, "Stand thou there, or sit here under my footstool."

But James asks, "Are ye not then partial in yourselves, and are become judges of evil thoughts? . . . If ye have respect to persons, ye commit sin, and are convinced of the law as transgressors" (2:4, 9).

In I Timothy 6:1-12 the same subject is dealt with and the young man Timothy is warned that "the love of money is the root of all evil: which while some coveted after, they have erred from the faith, and pierced themselves through with many sorrows" (v. 10).

There can be no greater tragedy than that of a soul-winner whose motives and ministry are affected by material gain or social betterment.

Social distinctions of this kind inevitably lead some soul-winners into the temptation of

2. Social defeatism

The very existence of social distinctions can create in some

Christian workers a sense of social defeatism. Instead of viewing men and women—religious or irreligious, intellectual or simple, rich or poor, cultured or uncultured—as sinners, all needing the Saviour, they allow the superficial distinctions of men to defeat the outworking of God's redeeming love, which saves without respect of persons.

The Bible says, "For there is no difference: for all have sinned, and come short of the glory of God. . . . For there is no difference between the Jew and the Greek: for the same Lord over all is rich unto all that call upon him. For whosoever shall call upon the name of the Lord shall be saved" (Romans 3:22, 23; 10:12, 13).

No honest soul-winner will deny the fact that there have been occasions when he has been paralyzed by a sense of defeatism, when contemplating an approach to someone intellectually above him, or perhaps someone socially beneath him. The temptation to be defeated by who people are, or what people are, must be overcome by the Spirit of power, as well as by the gospel of power.

Anticipating the preaching of the gospel in Rome, where there was every distinction conceivable, Paul could say, "I am not ashamed of the gospel of Christ: for it is the power of God unto salvation to every one that believeth" (Romans 1:16).

If the enemy of souls does not attack us along the lines of spiritual temptations and social temptations, then he will employ

III. THE SEXUAL TEMPTATIONS OF THE SOUL-WINNER

This kind of temptation is not sufficiently studied and mastered in Christian circles today, with the result that tragedy after tragedy occurs.

There are two principal aspects of sexual temptation in the work of soul-winning:

1. The temptation to ignore sex appeal

There are still well-intentioned Christian people who think that, because they now serve the Master, the factor of sex appeal no longer enters into their thinking, speaking, or acting. As a consequence of this, they face the danger of being defenseless against sexual temptation, and are often involved in sin—in thought if not in deed (see Matthew 5:27, 28).

That great soul-winner, the Apostle Paul, realized the importance of keeping under the body. Listen to his words of personal discipline as recorded in I Corinthians 9:27, "I keep under my body, and bring it into subjection: lest that by any means, when I have preached to others, I myself should be a castaway."

J. B. Phillips renders these words as follows, "I am my body's sternest master, for fear that, when I have preached to others, I should myself be disqualified [that is, disqualified for service; the salvation of the soul is not in view here]."

Without such self-mastery or personal discipline, even the Christian worker can be involved in moral sin. Intimate contact with people cannot be entertained without involving the factor of sex appeal; hence the need for watchfulness, discipline, and mastery.

2. The temptation to incite sex appetite

In I Thessalonians 4:3-6, the Apostle Paul is addressing Christian men and women when he says, "This is the will of God, even your sanctification, that ye should abstain from fornication: that every one of you should know how to possess his vessel in sanctification and honour; not in the lust of concupiscence, even as the Gentiles which know not God; that no man go beyond and defraud his brother in any matter:

because that the Lord is the avenger of all such, as we also have forewarned you and testified."

God's purpose for His people, and especially His servants, is that in all social relationships our bodies are to be possessed and preserved in sanctification and honor. That is to say, our bodies are to be separated unto God, and made to appear honorable before men.

This manner of living certainly involves the discipline of sex appetites. The Scripture we have just read warns that no man should defraud his brother in this matter of inciting sex appetite.

The Greek word used here suggests three ways in which sex appetite can be incited:

a. *By defrauding,* that is, exciting hungers which cannot be honorably satisfied.

b. *By oppressing,* that is, exerting a superior and more forceful personality over a weaker one, until it is sapped of initiative, individuality, and vitality.

c. *By overreaching,* that is, exceeding the laws of chastity and holiness until there is disaster.

Unless we are on our guard, it is perilously possible to defraud, oppress, or overreach, even in the work of soul-winning. This applies not only to the relationships of opposite sexes but also to those of the same sex. To behave in this fashion is to be judged by God, for "the Lord is the avenger of all such."

To be armed against sexual temptation in the work of soul-winning, there is negative as well as positive instruction in the Word of God:

(1) *The negative instruction.* ". . . make not provision for the flesh, to fulfil the lusts thereof" (Romans 13:14). And again, "Flee . . . youthful lusts" (II Timothy 2:22).

In our thinking, speaking, and acting, we are to be ever

watchful of anything that makes provision for the fulfilling of fleshly lusts. And when necessary, we are to flee from them.

(2) *The positive instruction.* "Walk in the Spirit, and ye shall not fulfil the lust of the flesh" (Galatians 5:16).

To know the conscious and constant fullness of the Holy Spirit in our lives, especially when engaged in the sacred work of winning men and women to Christ, is the secret of possessing our vessels in sanctification and honor. *Only the Holy Spirit can sanctify sex appeal and sublimate sex appetite.* When He fills the life, we know what it is to be separated unto God and made honorable before men.

We have seen the peculiar temptations that beset the soulwinner in his endeavor to seek and find men and women for Christ. How relevant, then, is the apostle's word to us when he says, "Wherefore let him that thinketh he standeth take heed lest he fall. There hath no temptation taken you but such as is common to man: but God is faithful, who will not suffer you to be tempted above that ye are able; but will with the temptation also make a way to escape, that ye may be able to bear it" (I Corinthians 10:12, 13).

Let us ever lean heavily on the faithfulness of God, and watch carefully for His way of escape, lest having preached to others we should be disqualified at the judgment seat of Christ.

THE SOUL-WINNER'S TRIUMPHS

Scriptures for Study

Furthermore, when I came to Troas to preach Christ's gospel, and a door was opened unto me of the Lord,

I had no rest in my spirit, because I found not Titus my brother: but taking my leave of them, I went from thence into Macedonia.

Now thanks be unto God, which always causeth us to triumph in Christ, and maketh manifest the savour of his knowledge by us in every place.

For we are unto God a sweet savour of Christ, in them that are saved, and in them that perish:

To the one we are the savour of death unto death; and to the other the savour of life unto life. And who is sufficient for these things?

For we are not as many, which corrupt the word of God: but as of sincerity, but as of God, in the sight of God speak we in Christ.

—II CORINTHIANS 2:12-17

Chapter 10

THE SOUL-WINNER'S TRIUMPHS

WHATEVER TRIALS AND TEMPTATIONS may beset the soul-winner, he can always know what it is to triumph. His attitude should be that of the great apostle when he exclaimed, "Thanks be unto God, which always causeth us to triumph in Christ, and maketh manifest the savour of his knowledge by us in every place" (II Corinthians 2:14).

Paul was on one of his soul-winning journeys when he gave expression to these words. He had intended to travel from Ephesus to Troas, to preach the gospel. In fact, he had arrived at Troas and a wonderful door of opportunity had been opened to him. But this pioneer evangelist was troubled and restless in his spirit. He had hoped to meet Titus at Troas, and learn from him the latest news of the disturbing happenings that were taking place in the church at Corinth. But Titus was nowhere to be found; so, leaving Troas, Paul proceeded into Macedonia, where he apparently found Titus. What his colleague had to tell him so thrilled his heart that he burst into this glorious doxology. In effect he said: "The Lord has scored another victory; rejoice with me. 'Thanks be unto God, which always causeth us to triumph in Christ.'"

For successful soul-winning, one must be able to react equally to situations of apparent failure or success with the song of triumph.

Such victorious soul-winning implies

I. SHARING A TRIUMPHANT FREEDOM IN CHRIST

Weymouth renders Paul's words thus: "To God be the thanks who in Christ ever leads us in His triumphal procession, displaying everywhere through us the sweetness of the knowledge of Him."

There seems to be no doubt that the apostle is employing in this verse the figure of a Roman triumph. While he had not yet been to Rome, Paul doubtless had heard of the great celebration days, when conquerors returned to the city and were watched by the emperor and the thronging crowds, as the victorious army paraded solemnly, yet gloriously, down the great Via Sacra* to the Capitoline Hill.

G. Campbell Morgan points out that, in such a Roman triumph, the conspicuous figures were those of the victors and the vanquished. The victor rode in triumph; the vanquished were often chained to the chariot wheels; and the whole procession was accompanied by the burning of incense. "Without dogmatizing," Dr. Morgan adds, "I believe that Paul here was viewing those engaged in the [gospel] ministry as the victors . . . describing their work as that of a triumphal march; and the vanquished, those . . . they had mastered [who were] accompanying on the march."

In these processional marches, there were two categories of prisoners:

1. The commended prisoners

These were men (and even women), who had accepted the conquest of their masters and were rejoicing as they moved along, chained to the chariot wheels. On the great day of the procession, the commended prisoners were always set free. But they never went home. They stayed with their masters

*The principal street of ancient Rome.

and would not return to their own country. In the language of the slave of the Old Testament, their decision would be: "I love my master . . . I will not go out free" (Exodus 21:5).

This is one of the joys of every soul-winner—when he returns from his soul-winning opportunities, with prisoners for Jesus Christ chained to the chariot wheels! There is no joy in Christian work like that of returning from the scene of battle with victims hitherto bound by the enemy, now enslaved to Christ. There is no greater freedom than that of captivity to Jesus Christ.

George Matheson expresses it beautifully in his hymn:

> Make me a captive, Lord,
> And then I shall be free;
> Force me to render up my sword,
> And I shall conqueror be.

In Paul's day, those commended prisoners realized that their conquerors were leading them into a new experience of life. Many of them hailed from downtrodden tribes, and, therefore, were only too glad to be freed by a great power like that of Rome.

In a similar way, men and women who are set free from Satan's bondage welcome the privilege of being mastered by the King of kings and Lord of lords, for His service is perfect freedom.

Then there were

2. The condemned prisoners

These were rebellious captives who, on that very account, were marked out for life imprisonment or execution. It is solemn yet necessary for the soul-winner to recognize that, if he is to follow in the train of the Saviour's triumph, the effect of his witness to the conquering Saviour will mean commendation for those who accept Christ and condemnation for those who reject Him. In either case, the triumphant freedom in Christ is celebrated and God is glorified.

Victorious soul-winning, in the next place, means

II. SHEDDING A TRIUMPHANT FRAGRANCE OF CHRIST

"For," declares the apostle, "we are a fragrance of Christ grateful to God in those being saved and in those perishing; to the one an odour of death that leads to death, and to others an odour of life that leads to life" (II Corinthians 2:15, 16, Weymouth).

In these triumphal processions, the prisoners carried censers of burning incense. As they waved them to and fro, the fragrance was diffused throughout the city, and everybody knew that the victors with their vanquished were marching down the Via Sacra.

We, too, as soul-winners share in a triumphal march, and as the incense ascends,

1. The name of our conquering Lord is exalted

His name is "as ointment poured forth" (Song of Solomon 1:3). His name spells salvation and deliverance, for at His birth the angel announced, "Thou shalt call his name JESUS: for he shall save his people from their sins" (Matthew 1:21).

And later, Peter could declare in one of his sermons, "There is none other name under heaven given among men, whereby we must be saved" (Acts 4:12).

It is the name of exaltation and triumph, for "God also hath highly exalted him, and given him a name which is above every name: that at the name of Jesus every knee should bow, of things in heaven, and things in earth, and things under the earth; and that every tongue should confess that Jesus Christ is Lord, to the glory of God the Father" (Philippians 2:9-11).

Nothing should thrill our hearts more than to hear those who have been captured for Christ acclaiming His rights, doing Him honor, exulting in His glories, speaking well of His character and courage, and magnifying the name which is above every name.

2. The fame of our conquering Lord is extended

Every prisoner chained to the chariot wheels extends the fame of our Saviour. The more prisoners there are, the greater the volume of incense that wafts afar the fame of this One who saves without respect of persons. They may be rich or poor, wise or simple, young or old.

> Red and yellow, black and white—
> All are precious in His sight.

John the Seer envisages such a scene as this in a day yet to come, when captives to Jesus Christ shall sing a new song, saying, "Thou art worthy . . . for thou wast slain, and hast redeemed us to God by thy blood out of every kindred, and tongue, and people, and nation; and hast made us unto our God kings and priests: and we shall reign on the earth" (Revelation 5:9, 10).

And again, "Worthy is the Lamb that was slain to receive power, and riches, and wisdom, and strength, and honour, and glory, and blessing" (Revelation 5:12).

This ascending fragrance will be the savor of life unto life to those who have capitulated to the sovereignty of Christ; and, alas, the savor of death unto death to those who have rejected Him, saying, "We will not have this man to reign over us" (Luke 19:14). The condemned prisoners, having reached the foot of the Capitoline Hill, were ushered into an underground prison. To them the wafted incense was an odor of death unto death. Once again, terrifying as this thought is, it must always be accepted in the context of the Saviour's triumph.

So our soul-winning is not only the sharing of a triumphant freedom in Christ, and the shedding of a triumphant fragrance of Christ; it also constitutes

III. SHOWING A TRIUMPHANT FAITHFULNESS TO CHRIST

The apostle goes on to say, "We are not as many, which corrupt the word of God: but as of sincerity, but as of God, in the sight of God speak we in Christ [of Christ]" (II Corinthians 2:17).

As we follow in the train of the Saviour's triumph, sharing as victors with Him, we show forth our loyalty to

1. The message of the gospel

"We are not as many, which corrupt the word." The idea implicit in the word "corrupt" was that of hucksters, or tavern traffickers. These people kept saloons and were notorious for adding water to the wine, thus corrupting or diluting it, and therefore making money under false pretenses.

Paul was aware of the presence in the Church of compromising teachers and evangelists who dared to adulterate or water down the Word of the gospel.

Here is a temptation to which any soul-winner might succumb; but to do so is to cease to move in the train of the Saviour's triumph.

The joy of soul-winning is not only that of seeing men and women saved through the power of the gospel but also of watching the converts "grow in grace and in the knowledge of our Lord and Saviour Jesus Christ" (II Peter 3:18).

The saintly John could say, "I have no greater joy than to hear that my children walk in truth" (III John 4).

God make us ever faithful to the message of the gospel.

Triumphant soul-winning, however, implies loyalty, not only to the message of the gospel, but also to

2. The ministry of the gospel

Notice how our text continues: ". . . as of sincerity . . . in the sight of God speak we in Christ" (II Corinthians 2:17). J. B. Phillips renders it ". . . in the Name of God, under the eyes of God, as Christ's chosen minister."

As soul-winners we have a wonderful ministry. With all its joys and sorrows, trials and triumphs, we are solemnly responsible to men and accountable to God. Like the elders referred to in Hebrews 13:17, we "watch for . . . souls, as they that must give account," that we "may do it with joy, and not with grief."

Looking back on his soul-winning work in the city of Thessalonica—with heaven in view—Paul could say, "What is our hope, or joy, or crown of rejoicing? Are not even ye in the presence of our Lord Jesus Christ at his coming? For ye are our glory and joy" (I Thessalonians 2:19, 20).

Surely, to present to the Master in glory men and women we have won here on earth must be the crowning joy and triumph of all soul-winning. Conversely, can there be any greater embarrassment or shame than to have to face the judgment seat of Christ empty-handed, without one soul with whom to greet Him?

What an incentive this is to be loyal to the ministry of the gospel day by day, until we see our Saviour face to face!

We have seen, then, that the triumphs of the soul-winner are those of sharing a freedom in Christ, shedding a fragrance of Christ, and showing a faithfulness to Christ in the endeavor to be a successful soul-winner.

BIBLIOGRAPHY

CHAFER, LEWIS SPERRY, *True Evangelism.* Findlay, Ohio: Dunham Publishing Company, 1919. False forces in evangelism; Biblical requirements for true evangelism.

HARRISON, EUGENE MYERS, and WILSON, WALTER L., *How to Win Souls.* Wheaton, Illinois: Scripture Press, 1952. Qualifications, message, and methods of the soul-winner; how to organize and conduct a crusade of personal witnessing in a local church.

MACAULAY, J. C., and BELTON, ROBERT H., *Personal Evangelism.* Chicago: Moody Press, 1956. Qualifications; how to deal with different classes, including some cults; excellent for Bible schools, evangelists, pastors, etc.; used as textbook at Moody Bible Institute.

SANDERS, J. O., *The Divine Art of Soul-Winning.* New York: Fleming H. Revell Company, 1937. Qualifications; how to deal with various classes, including some cults.

SPURGEON, C. H., *The Soul-Winner.* Grand Rapids, Michigan: Zondervan Publishing House, 1895. Qualifications; how to win souls; the cost and the reward of being a soul-winner.

TORREY, R. A., *How to Bring Men to Christ.* New York: Fleming H. Revell Company, 1893. Qualifications; how to deal with different classes.

TRUMBULL, CHARLES G., *Taking Men Alive.* New York: Fleming H. Revell Company, 1920. The work, the worker; how our Lord worked.

WHITESELL, FARIS D., *Great Personal Workers.* Chicago: Moody Press, 1956. Brief biographical sketches.